Measuring the Process: Guidelines for Evaluating Social Development

David Marsden
Peter Oakley
Brian Pratt

AN INTRAC PUBLICATION
1994

INTRAC:
Supporting the development of NGOs internationally

A SUMMARY DESCRIPTION
Set up in 1991 to provide specially designed Management Training & Research Services for European NGOs involved in Relief and Development in the South and dedicated to improving organisational effectiveness and programme performance of Northern NGOs and Southern partners where appropriate.

Our goal is to serve NGOs in (i) the exploration of the management, policy and human resource issues affecting their own organisational development, and (ii) the evolution of more effective programmes of institutional development and cooperation.

INTRAC offers the complementary services of
Training,
Consultancy
and Research

Within three themes

(1) NGO Management and Organisation
(2) Improving Development Projects and Programmes
(3) Media Management and Policy Advocacy

INTRAC is supported by the Aga Khan Foundation, UK

INTRAC
PO BOX 563
Oxford OX2 6RZ
UK

Telephone: 44 (0)865 201851
FAX: 44 (0)865 201852

Designed and produced by
Davies Burman Associates 0865 250079

Printed in Great Britain

ISBN 1 897748 06 X

CONTENTS

CHAPTER ONE

INTRODUCTION

The 'participatory' agenda that has gained prominence in thinking about development projects over the past decade gradually emerged as a result of the general disquiet felt about the effectiveness of development projects generally. The 'top down' interpretation of events and activities which characterised their appraisal, implementation and evaluation, left little space and little voice for the views of the recipients of aid flows. A focus on strategies for targeting and destroying poverty ignored the more generic structural inequities which perpetuated unequal relationships within and between communities. A search for the operationalisation of more participatory strategies which would centrally involve those who were perceived to be the objects of development efforts intensified.

As a result of discussions emerging from a series of workshops organised jointly by FAO and GTZ in Germany in the mid 1980s, a group of individuals proposed to take these problematic issues of representation and participation further. The group focused on evaluation on the premise that evaluations themselves provided important moments in the lives of all development projects, when opportunities for the 'negotiation of values' might be centrally addressed. To see evaluations as negotiating points in the process of development offered opportunities for furthering our understanding of the operationalisation of a participatory agenda and of building blocks in the development of effective partnerships between donor agencies and recipient institutions and communities.

There were few examples of the ways in which participation had been effectively incorporated into practice. The intention of the group was to bring together examples of successful practice and to disseminate such examples more widely. This was to be achieved through a workshop which brought together governmental and non-governmental organisations from different parts of the world to share experiences and, if possible, to enhance clarity of practice. Shared lessons would result in a sounder understanding of how the participatory agenda might be furthered. The initial workshop, entitled the 'International Workshop on the Evaluation of Social Development Projects', was held in Swansea, South Wales in September 1989.

The Swansea Workshop

The Swansea workshop brought together approximately 80 participants from a variety of Northern and Southern NGOs, from governments of the North and from multi-national development agencies. The results of that particular workshop were written up and published by Oxfam in 1990 (see Marsden and Oakley 1990).

A major focus of that initial workshop was on process projects which were concerned with trying to clarify how such things as capacity building, the achievement of self reliance, empowerment and sustainability might be understood more clearly. Consequently the issues of how these processes might be measured, who should be involved with that measurement, when were the optimum times to carry out these measurements, which methods should be used and why evaluations were being called for, were prominent in the discussions. Major emphasis was placed on the clarification of the objectives for evaluations. A constant theme underlying these discussions was a desire to negotiate ways in which value might be analysed. This was informed by a recognition of the problems associated with the search for universal solutions in the face of a need to ensure that local value systems and sensibilities were not ignored. Indeed one of the major tenets of any social development project was seen to be the central focus given to the involvement of 'beneficiaries' or project participants.

The workshop was further structured around four major themes. First of all, there was a focus on the development of more appropriate indicators for the evaluation of social development projects. Much attention has been given in recent years to the provision of more precise and objectively verifiable indicators in the pursuit of value for money and in attempts to understand more fully the ways in which interventions in the name of progress contribute to development. Secondly, there was a focus on the methodologies that might be most appropriate for the measurement of process; were such methodologies qualitatively distinct from more traditional quantitative measures? Thirdly, given the underlying concern to enhance participatory processes and involve the 'grass roots' more centrally in all aspects of decision making, there was a major discussion about the problems surrounding the development of 'partnerships' between donors and recipients. And, fourthly, given the renegotiation of the development agenda, there was concern to investigate the role and position of the evaluator. Major questions about the distinctions made between 'insiders' and 'outsiders' in a renegotiated relationship were raised.

While, as an introduction, an attempt was made at the workshop to define the parameters of social development, it was argued that any definition must be related to the context in which it is used. Social development was seen generally as implying an overall concern with the improvement and enhanced sustainability of individual and communal livelihoods within an equitable and fair social, economic and political system, rather than something different and separate from economic development. It also addresses sustainable local capacity building, access to resources by the poor in particular, and issues surrounding enabling and empowering. Two complementary themes formed a basis for all discussions. One theme focused on seeking to further an understanding of evaluation as a process of empowerment. The other theme focused on the search for more appropriate instruments of assessment, and on how to provide reliable evidence of positive change.

In conclusion the workshop emphasised that evaluation should be a learning process which was of value to the whole project community (including all stakeholders). Its aim should be the building and supporting of organic institutions. It was emphasised that evaluations necessarily involve different sets of understandings which would need to be negotiated, and that different methodologies would need to be adopted, not only in relation to the different contexts in which evaluations were called for, but also in terms of the different stakeholders with an interest in the process. The negotiation and clarification of objectives are an important part of this learning process and it was stressed that evaluations should be developmental rather than judgemental.

Box 1.1
Major Issues arising from the Evaluation
of Social Development

1. A Consumer Orientation
2. The Development of Quality Control Measures
3. Changing Organisational requirements
4. A Balance between Quantitative and Qualititative measures
5. The Need for Relevant/Timely/Accurate Information
6. Setting Clear Objectives
7. Achieving Realistic Targets
8. Building Management Information Systems

Arising from such conclusions, it was apparent that there was a need to investigate further possible, ways of re-aligning the relationships between donors and beneficiaries; a need to address the issues of accountability and legitimacy in multi-cultural contexts where different value systems prevailed; and a consequent need for evaluations to develop a community of interest with common purpose which built trust and mutual confidence. As a complement to more traditional and technocratic approaches to evaluation, it was suggested that an interpretative approach might be developed which, while constructively critical in its focus, demonstrated a reflexive awareness which addressed the extent to which objectivity was attainable and or desirable in achieving a balance between qualitative and quantitative measurements. A critical focus would revolve around the questioning of legitimacy and authority and of challenging unquestioned orthodoxy. An interpretative approach would aim to open up spaces for the development of dialogue between formerly unequal 'partners'. The workshop recognised that evaluations would not and could never be neutral because they were fundamentally concerned with control over direction and resources.

Following from the 1989 workshop, the debate about the evaluation of social development projects was taken forward through contributions made. to the Annual Conference of the Development Studies Association in 1991. Participants at the first workshop felt that the results, as expressed in the Oxfam publication, while useful, were somewhat inaccessible and did not adequately focus on practice. It was also felt that the workshop focused too narrowly on projects, to the exclusion of the wider contexts in which particular evaluations were embedded. Evaluation should also look at the suitability of particular sorts of organisations for achieving social development objectives. An analysis of organisations might indicate more appropriate forms for the delivery of particular inputs and suggest ways in which restructuring to take account of such objectives might be achieved.

Box 1.2
The Process of Interpretative Evaluation

1. Identify the full range of interested parties
2. Find out how the evaluation is perceived—stakeholder claims and concerns
3. Provide a context and a methodology through which these can be understood, taken into account and constructively criticised
4. Generate as much consensus about different interpretations as possible
5. Prepare an agenda for negotiation
6. Collect and provide the information requested in the agenda
7. Establish and mediate a forum of stakeholders in which negotiation can take place
8. Develop a text available to all
9. Recycle evaluation to take up unresolved issues

The Amersfoort Workshop

A second International Workshop was held in Amersfoort, The Netherlands, in May 1992, to take some of these issues forward. It was intended to build on the outcomes of the earlier workshop and developments in the field over the intervening period. While the aim of the first workshop was primarily conceptual in nature and attempted to highlight the key dimensions of the process of evaluation of social development, the second workshop was more concerned with the detail of practice through the examination of a number of commissioned case studies. It aimed to identify key aspects and methodologies associated with an emerging practice, and to develop appropriate guidelines, in a text that might provide a reference point for agencies involved in the evaluation of social development projects and programmes. Another key aim was to identify areas of evaluation which demand further examination and which could constitute an agenda for future research. Since 1992 Save the Children Fund has been developing an evaluation 'tool kit' (see SCF 1994) which goes some way towards providing such a text. It is hoped that this synthesis of the Amersfoort workshop can complement the SCF production and those operational manuals produced by AGKED and MISEREOR (1991), COTA (see Beaudoux et al. 1992), Pratt and Loizos (1992) and ODA (1993a) and further the debate about the measurement of social development.

About 18 months prior to the workshop, participants were given a framework which was considered practical for presenting their experiences and which was to be used as a guide in the construction of contributions. The framework emphasised four principle stages in the construction of an evaluation—preparation, execution, analysis and reflection. The aim was to try and develop a basis from which the different experiences might be compared. Firstly, presenters were asked to briefly describe the project or programme to be evaluated. Secondly, they were asked to address the question of who called for the evaluation and why. Thirdly, they were asked to describe the methodology and the data collection techniques used. In addition they were asked how the findings were produced and discussed, and to reflect on the ways in which the evaluation data was used. While some of the case studies adopted this framework in the presentation of their findings, others did not keep to the framework.

Three basic objectives were set for this second workshop: firstly, to examine practice and to identify key aspects of, and methodologies for practice; secondly to embark on the construction of a set of guidelines for the evaluation of social development projects and build up a typology of different methods; and thirdly, to identify key areas for further examination. Although the continuity of participants attending both workshops was less than hoped for, this did not impair the ability to build on the debates and questions raised by the first workshop. Participants came with a variety of objectives including some expectations that the workshop would provide a training forum for those wishing to know 'how to do it'. This was not the aim.

Over 30 participants from a variety of non-governmental organisations and academic institutions were represented at the workshop. A full list of participants with their organisational affiliations is given at the end of the text. The workshop was divided into plenary sessions at the beginning and the end. Participants were split into three groups to examine particular case studies prepared for the workshop and were each asked to focus on one of the three major themes that the workshop was attempting to develop. One group focused on the issues surrounding the purposes, the preparation and the timing of evaluations. A second group focused on the problems surrounding the choice of methodologies. The third group analysed the uses to which evaluations of social development projects might be put, with a focus on questions of interpretation, translation, negotiation and dissemination.

Like the text from the Swansea workshop, this text does not attempt to reproduce the proceedings; rather it attempts to synthesise the major issues which emerged from the five day meeting and to identify the major themes debated. It also attempts to suggest ways in which future work might be taken up. Chapter 2 provides a partial literature review of material that has fed into the current analysis in one way or another. Chapter 3 consists of three of the case studies presented at the workshop and summaries of the discussions of the major issues raised by them. Chapter 4 examines a variety of approaches to the evaluation of social development. Chapter 5 provides a preliminary set of guidelines for such evaluations. This is followed by a concluding chapter which attempts to draw the various threads together and point the way towards future developments in this important field.

We would like to thank all those who contributed in one way or another to the development of the workshop. Particular thanks are due to those organisations which provided financial support in addition to sending representatives. These are Christian Aid, Norwegian Church Aid, CAFOD, CEBEMO, AGKED and MISEREOR, and the Save the Children Fund. Without their support it would have been impossible to ensure the wide representation of representatives of non-government organisations from the South. Hans Knuvener, head of evaluation at MISEREOR, and Tony Fernandes remained as members of the advisory group that was responsible for the thinking behind both the first and the second workshop.

David Mansfield was responsible for the first draft of Chapter 2 and we acknowledge with thanks the considerable effort he put into that work. Maria Ribeiro was responsible for the stream-lined administration which she appeared to handle effortlessly. Andrew Clayton at INTRAC has pushed and cajoled the authors to bring the text together and is responsible for the formidable editing task that was involved in bringing it to publication. We would also wish to extend our sincere thanks to all the participants at the workshop. We have attempted to synthesise some very important debates and hope that we have been able to do justice to them. Like the participatory production of a single agreed text that was recommended as the favoured product of a participatory process, we feel that attribution of individual authorship is not without its problems. This is particularly so for a work of this kind. We hope that we have been able to provide a suitable lens through which the practical work of others might be more clearly seen, and while acknowledging our debt to others, we apologise to those who do not feel as though they have been fairly represented.

David Marsden, Peter Oakley and Brian Pratt
OXFORD, February 1994

CHAPTER TWO

THE EVALUATION OF SOCIAL DEVELOPMENT: A REVIEW OF THE CURRENT LITERATURE

Introduction

The purpose of this literature review, like the evaluation process itself, is to facilitate the dissemination of information which, in turn, will help to both inform practice and build consensus. While it does not claim to be comprehensive, the review does attempt to cover a range of literature which deals in one form or another with the evaluation of social development. The review tries to highlight recent work which moves away from more traditional forms of evaluation and to uncover the problems associated with an emergent practice which occupies more and more organisations in their search for 'best practice'.

With the proliferation of projects aimed at implementing social and cultural change, and with increased attention being given to the micro-level effects of macro-level economic policies in the past decade or so, the validity of conventional methods of evaluation has come under much scrutiny. This has been particularly noticeable in the various attempts to deal with the social dimensions of structural adjustment programmes (see Cornia *et al.* 1987, World Bank 1991, UNDP 1993). It is also highlighted by recent interest in the importance of incorporating a cultural dimension into analyses of development and change (see Verhelst 1990 for example).

Furthermore the inability of methods such as social cost-benefit analysis and social impact assessment to accurately and adequately reflect the dynamics of such changes has resulted in increasing calls for the involvement of those more aware of, and better able to explain, qualitative developments: i.e. the so-called 'project beneficiaries' themselves. The extent of this involvement or 'participation' and how it is utilised, is at the heart of the debate concerning the evaluation of social development and at the heart of the debate surrounding issues such as empowerment.

A recognition of the current importance attached to social development is given by the fact that the UN is organising a major conference on that subject in 1994. An attempt to define the parameters of social development was made in the first workshop on the 'Evaluation of Social Development Projects' held in September 1989 (Marsden and Oakley 1990). Social development is not an alternative to economic development. It is the

9

incorporation of a more 'people-oriented' focus into general development efforts. Such a 'people oriented' focus has been discussed and elaborated extensively over the past decade (see Cernea 1985, Chambers 1985, Rahman 1984, Khan 1983 and Oakley 1991 for example) and has now entered the mainstream of thinking about the purposes and objectives of interventions in the name of development. A very useful review of developments in the appraisal, monitoring and evaluation of British NGO projects and of the theoretical and practical changes in thinking about development interventions is to be found in Howes (1991).

Social Development and Empowerment

Social development projects seek to give support to self reliant strategies, to promote more effective participation, to build local capacity, and to develop skills for more sustainable development. A fundamental issue underpinning this notion of social development is that of empowerment. Empowerment, together with self reliance, sustainability and participation, are very difficult concepts to define. Indeed these catch-all terms are seen by some now as of little value in the pursuit of specificity and clarity. But in their ambiguity lies their strength. Consisting as they do of a variable set of objectives which depend on different value premises for their understanding, they may be interpreted in a variety of ways. Their use prevents closure and capture and provides the well-springs for renewed creativity. A recent publication by John Friedman (1992) entitled *Empowerment: the Politics of Alternative Development*, for example, examines some of these issues but with specific relationship to realities in South America. Friedman's text is an important contribution to the debate since it not only examines in some detail the historical roots of the empowerment issue but, in similar detail, also examines the emerging practice.

At the root of these concepts is the aim of building sustainable assets, both human and physical, and of transferring resources, responsibility and ownership to those who have hitherto been excluded from development efforts–the poor and the marginalised–because they are seen to have been disadvantaged by social, economic and political changes. A parallel aim is the building of partnerships with the poor to enrich the networks and alliances that link North and South. Behind the concepts lie philosophical debates about justice and equity. They are the battle fronts for competing claims for authority and legitimacy in a constantly changing world.

Management and Institutional Capacity Building

The means whereby resources and responsibilities can be built up and/or transferred are seen to lie primarily in institution- and capacity-building. In order to increase the chances for longer term sustainability of development initiatives and to decrease dependency and the dangers of exploitation, strong community-based organisations (CBOS) are required. This institution- and capacity-building extends however from CBOS through to the organisations associated with the transfer of resources from the North to the South. As such, management capacity building programmes to increase the effectiveness of organisations at all levels (international aid agencies, national bureaucracies, Southern NGOs, and village level institutions) are an integral part of these developments.

It is argued that unless this process of social development takes place then many if not all development efforts are likely to be unsustainable once the development project is completed. But how can objectives such as those enshrined in social development processes be appropriately measured? How can one understand such increased responsibility, such enhanced sustainability? And what sorts of timing will be required in an era dominated by supposedly discrete 'project cycles'?

Transcending Sectoral Divides

Social development, like the work of many NGOs, typically crosses sectoral boundaries and thus sits uncomfortably with the efforts of many line ministries or sectorally specialised agencies. A recognition that development is cross-sectoral and multi-faceted leads to a search for indicators of achievement that transcend sectoral divides. Concern is not primarily with increased yields or with reduced mortality, but rather with the place of those achievements in a more holistic understanding of development. A focus on the environment, on women, on population, on poverty and on good governance affect all traditional sectoral foci, and demand different methodologies for the interpretation of achievement. They also demand the re-appraisal of existing policies to ensure that these more recent priorities for development policy are adequately incorporated. Current efforts, for example, by the ODA in Britain in the development of a Policy Information Marker System (PIMS) attempt to do this and thereby ensure that major policy objectives are given higher priority. The recent publication of the ODA's manual on social development goes some way to address these trans-sectoral issues (ODA 1993b).

Management and Evaluation

At the heart of social development efforts is the notion of increasing peoples' abilities to more effectively manage their own resources. The results of such efforts will be expected to enhance productive activity and social welfare generally. If interventions are to be sustainable in the longer term then people themselves must feel a sense of ownership and worth. This they will only do if they value positively what is being developed with them.

Management, the effective stewarding of scarce resources, would seem to have gained ascendancy over traditional economics as the focus for thinking about development. A review of evaluation of social development must thus incorporate some mention of the changes in management thinking that have taken place during the 1980s. The development of more flexible working conditions, the emergence of what one might call the 'contract culture', the retrenchment of public bureaucracies, focus more attention on the development of systems of measurement for the assessment of performance and on more sophisticated systems for appraising the value of activities and of individuals. The rise of private organisations and institutions whose primary objectives are not governed by a business culture or by the need to operate in a 'free market' demand different methods for measuring performance and success. The development of different methodologies for measuring achievement is highlighted by the recent experiments with social audit being undertaken by TraidCraft and the New Economics Foundation (see Zadek and Evans 1993).

When evaluation is undertaken in ways which enhance consensus then positive results are deemed to be forthcoming. When it is done with the aim of differentiating between people and organisations on the basis of cost-effectiveness criteria or improving efficiency through systematic performance appraisal, it is not guaranteed that it will be met with whole-hearted support. Conventional attitudes towards evaluation tend to be suspicious of management's motives in mounting evaluations. Among the stake-holders there are likely to be victims as well as beneficiaries.

The Chains that Bind

While the rhetoric of 'participation' and 'empowerment' inform the wider discussions of social development, we are still apparently chained to ways of thinking and acting which inhibit effective elaboration of successful methodologies. The restrictive heuristic devise incorporated, for example, into the 'project cycle' assumes that there should be a beginning and an end to the development intervention. The chains that still bind us to the search for objectivity and neutrality lead us back to thinking of evaluation 'naturally' taking place at the end of the project.

While we uphold ideas about projects as 'processes' or as 'policy experiments' (Rondinelli 1983), we are also constrained by rigid funding cycles, and demands for accountability and efficiency that are rooted in financial concerns and controls. There is an increased interest in measuring achievements, with ensuring accountability and transparency, and with meeting specific objectives. Notions of success remain largely unquestioned. The values which drive actions are less clear now than they were when the 'modernising mission' was taken for granted. It is deemed even more important now to achieve unambiguous clarity and focus, and to ensure that investments are getting to the right people and that they are being utilised effectively. But the search for quality measured in culturally relative terms remains illusive (but see Pirsig 1992 who provides a very thought provoking analysis of the problems associated with the search for quality).

Evaluation and Measurement

The evaluation process, when approached from what might be termed a traditional perspective, is understood as a retrospective review of what has happened in order to consolidate present or shift future directions of effort by measuring success and failure. This has usually meant the elaboration of suitable indicators of achievement by outsiders. In the private sector this is often measured with reference to financial profitability. On the other hand, in the public sector it has been measured by reference to progress in the various social sectors–health, education and provision of social services for the elderly and the disabled. In the not-for-profit sector other, often less tangible, measures of success are required. Evaluation as measurement also involves issues of control. Who decides what is to be measured and on the criteria whereby success is to be measured?

The search for appropriate indicators to measure the development process has been something that many have worked on over the last four decades. Most notably the United Nations Research Institute for Social Development undertook substantial research in the measurement of progress in social welfare and development (Ghai and Westendorff 1994, see also Hillhorst and Klatter 1985). This has been continued with the work of UNDP through its Human Development Report. But the main set of indicators of this type is still provided through the World Bank's annual Development Report. Measurements of achievements in the fields of health, education, housing and social welfare provision still provide the most widely used indicators of general social development. These focus on relatively easily obtainable sectoral information but they provide little information about the achievement of broader goals. Indicators for the measurement of environmental degradation, of good government, of institutional maturity, for example remain under-developed. (One interesting experiment on the production of an Institutional Maturity Index is currently being developed by the Aga Khan Rural Support Programme in the northern areas of Pakistan, see Aga Khan Rural Support Programme 1993.)

Evaluation as Interpretation

When approached from what might be termed an interpretative perspective, however, evaluation acquires a very different and more central function; one which questions the very nature of the premises on which the development project is based. This is perhaps why current evaluations so often begin by examining 'mission statements' of organisations and thereby clarifying objectives, and by calling for 'base-line' information from which estimations of success or failure can be made. In a changing world, evaluations become tools for 'rooting' current activities and redesigning inter-relationships. This examination of practice is a constant feature and the time bound activities of appraisal and monitoring become incorporated into the constant process associated with the analysis of value and quality, which are not seen as separate activities with time-bound parameters.

In an age when many of the cherished values which informed past western development efforts are being questioned there is an acknowledgement, on the one hand, of the relative importance of the values of others and, on the other hand, of the need to negotiate a consensus both over shared values in the search for a common humanity and with the emergence of a 'global culture' (see Featherstone 1990). Therein lies the dilemma for an interpretative evaluation. How can one impose a set of values associated with particular understandings of concepts such as accountability, effectiveness, and efficiency onto circumstances and conditions which are informed by sometimes contradictory sets of values? Western conceptions of the environment, for example, may reasonably be questioned by others who see themselves facing a very different set of problems. Western conceptions of equality do not necessarily fit easily into conditions where family obligations presume paternal authority. And who is the arbiter of what 'good government' should be? Different value systems reflect different priorities and if partnerships are to be developed which can accommodate those different sets of values, then methodologies need to be evolved that make those values explicit and inscribe them in public charters understood and agreed by all.

Evaluation as Critical Analysis

A common form of evaluation is that associated with academic enquiries of one sort or another. These are evaluations which are made by outsiders and which have no claim to be developing 'best practice'. They are not usually commissioned by project managers, but are often based on the results of some commissioned work. If we define evaluation as a tool of management then they are not strictly speaking evaluations at all. But their messages are clear. They seek to understand and to put values on different social, political, economic and cultural phenomena. Such evaluations are, perhaps, more correctly labelled critical analyses. They have been written by what some would term 'negative academics'. They are not meant either as tools for management, (although management will often use them) or to be read and understood by local beneficiaries of projects. They are, rather, reflections of an academic style of enquiry apparently divorced from practice. They purport to offer objective and dispassionate accounts of economic and social processes, but inevitably either consciously or unconsciously they offer different perspectives on those processes (which are often uncomfortable for managers). Nevertheless they provide important evaluations of the development process and need to be seriously considered as they often provide detailed historical and cultural descriptions of particular circumstances. Two good examples of recent publications in this field are Porter *et al.* (1991) and Ferguson (1990). Others do not conceal their biases against development efforts (c.f. Hancock 1989 and Morris 1991).

Critical studies of organisations involved in development are less common but the study by Van Ufford *et al.* (1988) of the tensions within a Dutch Development agency, the edited collections by Pottier (1993) and by Croll and Parkin (1992) respectively, and the forthcoming edited collection by Sue Wright, 'The Anthropology of Organisations', are notable sources of insight into the sociology and anthropology of organisations. Similarly, the work by Reed (1989 and 1992) on the sociology of management and of organisations provides important evaluations of current trends. Gasper's (1987) study of the politics of evaluation looks at the possible inter-personal tensions associated with evaluations. The work of Wildavsky (1979) on policy analysis, written some years ago now but still relevant, should also be mentioned in this connection.

Such analyses attempt to uncover the often 'hidden agendas' associated with the relationships between organisations and between individuals within organisations. They stress the importance of understanding the history of organisational development, and the culturally specific nature of much activity. They represent a style of analysis which is often difficult to incorporate directly into development projects. But just because they are difficult does not mean that they are unimportant. With current changes in the social sciences and questions about how ethnographies can be written and who the information is used by, issues of objectivity and subjectivity are raised as central questions. The distinctions between external (or 'etic') and internal (or 'emic') perspectives are called into question. Such questioning in academic circles is paralleled in the world of the development practitioner in the debates about the nature of the participation of the poor in development efforts.

Participation in Evaluation

The traditional types of evaluation were generated largely by the demands of management. They were closely associated with greater attempts at control over activities (and indirectly over personnel). They have undergone some significant changes in recent years. There has been a gradual evolution from what Guba and Lincoln (1989) refer to as first generation evaluation, or evaluation as measurement associated, among other things with scientific management, through second generation evaluation with the development of 'programme evaluation', to third generation evaluation with evaluation as judgement.

The evolution has been in the direction of incorporating beneficiaries more centrally into the evaluation process. But much of this effort has been associated with the refinement of ways of thinking which we referred to in 'The Evaluation of Social Development Projects' (Marsden and Oakley 1990) as technocratic. Guba and Lincoln point out the faults in such evaluations as 'a tendency toward managerialism, a failure to accommodate value-pluralism, and overcommitment to the scientific paradigm of enquiry' (1989:31–32).

The various publications of the American Evaluation Association and the extensive evaluation series, published by Sage, document developments in the United States over the last fifteen years (see in particular Patton 1978, 1980, 1981, 1982, and Guba and Lincoln 1989). They are not primarily directed at the evaluation of social development projects in the Third World, but need to be given more attention in the elaboration of new methodologies in that latter field. Many of their perspectives can be usefully incorporated into emerging methodologies. A concentration on utilisation-focused, qualitative, creative and practical evaluation points in the direction of evaluation methodologies which are more 'people-focused' and what are coming to be known as participatory evaluations.

From one perspective, and in the hands of some, participation in evaluation can be seen as merely the extension of ideas about modernisation: Third World countries are expected to emulate western practice; the extension and refinement of methodologies are aimed at more effectively managing organisations and resources in a changing world; and additional sorts of work are grafted onto existing frameworks without a recognition that their incorporation will involve structural changes. Such perspectives focus on management by objectives, on strategies for decision-making, on achieving high standards through 'quality assurance', and on appropriate organisational design.

Evaluation as Market Research

Evaluations can be seen as means of collecting more appropriate information in pursuit of more appropriate goals; of understanding the 'market' in order to target interventions more effectively. There are similarities with the techniques employed by market researchers to understand consumer preferences. Scarlett Epstein, for example, utilises market research for developmental purposes. She argues that by using conventional market research that is culturally adapted, beneficiaries' beliefs, perceptions and values can be elicited to ensure more 'user focused' interventions in a more efficient, effective and economical way. This process is similar to the use of opinion polls to uncover the views of the general public on political matters. Referring to citizens in the Third World, she writes:

> ... the major part of their development contribution rests in their intimate knowledge and understanding of existing practices, what improvements they would like and how these are likely to effect their lives. (Epstein 1992:5)

By utilising existing research followed by a process of qualitative enquiries and quantitative surveys of carefully sampled groups, developmental market research (DMR) is seen to give a voice to previously silent beneficiaries. Furthermore, given a conscientious selection of informants, representative of the heterogeneous nature of society, projections can be made to cover ever larger populations. Despite the criticisms that this work adopts a rather simplistic approach to culture, believing it possible to represent such a dynamic through a combination of key variables, it is Epstein's use of 'social marketing' that demonstrates the functionalist approach of her methods. Via the application of commercial marketing, it is suggested that the information gleaned from its participants can be utilised to produce 'socially desirable objectives' thereby playing an integral part in altering human behaviour. The precise nature of these 'objectives' are not really clarified and perhaps more importantly, it is never determined to whom they might be 'desirable'. As an attempt to bring cultural dimensions into decisions about marketing strategies she goes some way towards incorporating peoples' needs into the development equation.

The Evolution of Evaluation Perspectives

Parallel, but largely separate developments were taking place in the UK and western Europe at the beginning of the 1980s. The efforts surrounding the development of rapid appraisal methods (see Chambers et al. 1989), of putting farmers first in the design and implementation of rural development projects were particularly influential. Much of this early work was designed to tackle the twin constraints associated with lengthy social enquiries; the constraints of time and cost, and the 'outsider' bias associated with an unreflexive style of research. Attempts to combine the strengths of anthropological types of analysis with those of 'more rigorous' (deemed 'harder') research were being made. The judgement of the external evaluator was questioned as the importance of the 'beneficiary' and of anthropological and sociological perspectives became recognised (see Bamberger 1989, Cernea 1985). Unlike earlier attempts to attach importance to the social and cultural, which proceeded from a perspective which identified these fields as additional to economic analyses (see, for example, Cochrane 1979), these more recent analyses maintained that these dimensions were central to every sort of analysis.

Participation has increasingly become part of the conventional wisdom surrounding development projects. This can be seen as a partial consequence of donor agencies' seeking to achieve more efficient, effective and sustainable development interventions. In 1986 Feuerstein maintained that 'participatory evaluation' was, 'not intended to replace the more traditional evaluation methods. However, they can often make those methods that are useful more appropriate and effective' (1986:ix).

In this sense, participation has more often than not been associated with project planning and implementation and less frequently with evaluation. It is 'outsiders' using supposedly objective methods who have been responsible for the final decision on whether a project has succeeded in its pursuit of predetermined objectives. Participation in this form is therefore seen as functional to evaluation, assisting the 'expert' to come to a final decision. Its inclusion is essential if evaluation is to account fully for the qualitative changes that may or may not have taken place. The qualitative glosses that can be put on quantitative data provide opportunities for richer investigations of problematic areas revealed by that data.

The literature on this form of analysis is extensive and mainly focuses on how accurate information may be obtained in a cost effective and time efficient manner. Much of it concerns appraisal and monitoring as well as evaluation, but indicates the wide range of techniques and methodologies that may be utilised to elicit information from beneficiaries. The World Bank has been responsible for the production of an authoritative two volume study of project monitoring and evaluation in agriculture (see Casley and Kumar 1987 and 1988). The UN inter-agency task force on rural development, through its panel on monitoring and evaluation, prepared a set of guiding principles on the design and use of monitoring and evaluation in rural development projects and programmes in 1985 (see IFAD 1985). This also contains a list of references of separate UN agencies' monitoring and evaluation guidelines and handbooks as well as publications on that subject from the Asian Development Bank, the World Bank, USAID and the OECD from the late seventies and first part of the eighties.

Rethinking the Development Effort

The evolution in thinking about evaluation has been associated with a rethinking of the development effort and of the nature of relationships between donors and beneficiaries or recipients of aid. It has involved a rethinking of the whole nature of the way in which resources might be transferred, and incorporates the search for more appropriate organisational forms. This has been given added importance by the rapid development of NGOs with supposedly different agendas from those of governments and multi-national agencies.

It is often argued that because of the comparative smallness of such organisations they are more easily able to adapt to changing circumstances, and adopt new methods. It might be more appropriate to perceive NGOs in the light of a much wider evolution of thinking about the nature of the work of development organisations generally. This is associated with the changing role of governments in an era of economic liberalisation, with the development of the 'contract culture' referred to earlier, and with emerging understandings of how efficiency and effectiveness might be enhanced. It is not so much that NGOs are small and flexible, but that a changing appreciation of progress generally requires such a focus (see Handy 1988, and Nadler and Tushman 1988). The changing nature and focus of international agencies, such as the World Bank and UNDP as well as many of the UN agencies, implies, not just an overhauling of unresponsive bureaucracies, but also a shift in the ways in which they approach new development tasks.

The managerialist perspective that emerges is one of control by enlightened leaders aimed at achieving targets, building organisational capacity and of extending and processing information and knowledge within the organisation. An understanding of organisational culture is geared to the more effective utilisation of resources and achievement of strategic goals.

When transplanted into local organisational development in the Third World, issues of control and coordination tend to be ignored. Not only does the 'developed world' provide the role model in such a framework but also (through the influence of 'western expertise') the stimuli by which development might be fostered. The thrust of evaluations which adopt this perspective is to collect what is perceived to be more appropriate information. But the use of that information usually remains under the control of the outsider, the manager or the leader; to be used by management rather than by 'beneficiaries'.

Evaluation and Rates of Return on Investments

Evaluations that examine rates of return on investments proceed from a rather narrow set of principles rooted in western business practice. Such analyses assume that traditional methods can be extended to cover what are less tangible goals. With the rise of NGOs based on principles that do not enshrine the profit motive, the benefits of development assistance are increasingly seen in broader terms—organisational and institutional development, access to assets, resources and knowledge, and transparency and accountability. But while struggling with the needs for new forms of assessment criteria and new types of indicators that can measure success or failure, many NGOs are still constrained by the need to justify expenditure of public money in ways that are understandable and acceptable to financial auditors. They are also conscious of the need to obtain reliable information in a cost-effective manner.

While many acknowledge that traditional information gathering exercises which deliver quantitative results have problems attached to them, they do nevertheless provide tangible results that can, with caution, be successfully used by policy makers. The World Bank for example in a cost benefit analysis of a variety of development projects determined that those which included participation as a central element had a higher rate of return than those which did not; a result which suggests that participation is good for business.

The Evaluation of Povery Alleviation Projects

With concern expressed about the social consequences of structural adjustment programmes, increasing efforts have been made to measure the impact of macro-economic policy changes on local living standards. Efforts to ensure that 'safety nets' cushion those below the poverty line from their effects have involved the development of monitoring and evaluation systems in a number of countries to more effectively measure impact (see, for example, the Social Dimensions of Adjustment Programmes carried out in a number of African countries). This has also involved closer collaboration between international agencies, national governments and NGOs in developing more coordinated approaches to poverty reduction programmes. NGOs are seen as providing resources and expertise which governments, in an era of retrenchment, are unable to summon.

But the increased expectations from NGOs needs to be dealt with cautiously. Riddell argues that it is the raised profile of NGOs and the increased amount of public money channelled through them that has made evaluation essential to ensure that interventions are effective in alleviating poverty. Their grassroots bases and limited financial resources, 'provide reasons against NGOs departing radically from current practice and initiating a new and different, possibly expensive and potentially disruptive system of evaluation' (1990:9). What Riddell calls for is a change in present practice that will acknowledge the time, financial and skill constraints that NGOs operate under. The result is a cost-benefit analysis determined by the evaluator. This will consider what s/he perceives to be the relevant costs and benefits and the appropriate blend of quantitative and qualitative data necessary for an effective evaluation. Aimed primarily at determining the success or failure of poverty alleviation projects the emphasis of the evaluation is to provide the answers to a set of key questions. These questions consider the effectiveness of the project in improving the economic status of the beneficiaries, whether it could be made more efficient in achieving this, and the likelihood of successful replication. The approach suggested is based on building consensus. If there is little conflict between the relevant actors or groups affected by the evaluation then Riddell sees little purpose in adopting costly and time consuming techniques for verification.

Like Epstein, Riddell suggests both time and money should be saved by accessing existing information before any initial visit to the project site. For eliciting the views of those affected and involved in the project's implementation, a detailed 'hands-on' visit is advocated. But what Riddell considers to be the most important phase of evaluation is where initial conclusions are reached and any gaps in data are identified. Unlike conventional evaluation, the sharing of these judgements 'is a constituent part of the process of evaluation' (1990:20).

Although this method of evaluation could be perceived as more participatory than most, with its main objective being the pursuit of consensus, it is in fact a cost and time saving exercise. By seeking consensus on judgements made it is felt the assigning of values to qualitative data and the measuring of quantitative data becomes unimportant. The level of consensus reached will in turn determine whether it is actually necessary to collect further information given the time constraints that the evaluation is faced with. To decide this and the type of information required Riddell provides a matrix. Based on the nature of the 'evidence' and the potential to obtain 'better data' the onus is yet again on the evaluator to determine the pattern of events. Through interviews with beneficiaries, discussions with local government officials and project staff, and the use of secondary materials, the final information is collected and collated. The result of this is a project evaluation report as predetermined as the process that it evolved from:

> It is expected that the overall length of each project evaluation report, excluding the appendices but including the 2-3 page summary and the title page, would be around 25 pages of 1½-spaced A4 size paper. (Riddell 1990:27)

From his preliminary working paper a number of field evaluations have arisen. These have attempted to apply this broad framework in a range of projects aimed at raising the social and economic status of the poor in differing countries. These evaluations have sought to deal with what has been referred to as, 'a widespread assumption amongst official donors, and increasingly within government circles that NGOs are more successful in reaching the poor by virtue of being small-scale, flexible, innovative, participatory and low cost in their style of functioning' (Robinson 1992:118).

Robinson's paper (1992) concentrates on the practicalities of such an approach for the evaluation of an integrated rural development programme in coastal Andhra Pradesh. This conveys vividly the pros and cons of Riddell's attempt to develop a workable methodology that can bypass the debate over quantitative versus qualitative indicators. In the field such a method is depicted as having many of the problems of conventional evaluations: the absence of quantified data; problems of comparability; the influence of bias on qualitative data; and the isolation of project effects from those of external factors. White provides a fairly comprehensive coverage of the problems in undertaking such an enquiry in Bangladesh, concluding that, 'the significance of these points goes far beyond an explanation of difficulties in data collection; they indicate the world in which people live'(White 1991:96).

The Search for Replicability

The search for a 'blueprint' type approach to evaluate what are essentially complex processes is also dealt with by Paudyal (1991). He focuses on the need for a highly integrated and comprehensive monitoring and evaluation system that is capable of providing a broad base for effective management and the efficient use of resources. He provides a list of 26 proposed indicators for the monitoring and evaluation of agricultural reform (AR) and rural development (RD) projects as drawn up by the Centre for Integrated Rural Development for Asia and the Pacific (CIRDAP). Paudyal suggests that the use of such qualitative and quantitative indicators by the various implementing agencies involved in a project or programme would assist in providing a coordinating mechanism by which to consolidate both information gathering and cooperation.

Reviewing four Asian countries and their experiences of monitoring and evaluation mechanisms Paudyal believes the call for greater coordination stems from the need to eliminate any gaps in information that might exist. To ensure this a coordinating agency at the national level is recommended. Supported by the ministries and departments concerned, the indicators listed would provide the necessary information by which to assess interventions and intercede if required. By creating a more comprehensive data base from which to derive decisions, both government and implementing agencies are believed to obtain a greater understanding of the processes and causal factors involved in development interventions. Subsequently, participatory methods are seen only in the context of project based development and as insufficient for the broader framework on which macro decisions can be based.

Recent developments in the monitoring and evaluation work of the International Fund for Agricultural Development (IFAD) (see Spitz 1993), support the development of local level (regional or district) monitoring and evaluation units which can respond quickly to local changes of circumstances and generate much needed local information. While this is perceived apparently in terms of agricultural and environmental monitoring and evaluation, there is no reason to limit it to such physical data gathering. But, as with Paudyal's recommendations, attention needs to be given to the cost implications of such approaches, and the trade offs between timely and not so accurate information with those provided by these potentially very expensive methods.

Defining the Process of Evaluation

Over the past few years attempts have been made to encapsulate methods and approaches in guidelines and manuals for practitioners. While these are useful, they should not be treated as 'cookery books' with tried and trusted methods to be replicated anywhere and everywhere. As they distil experience, they inevitably take the reader away from specific realities by excluding detailed histories and cultures from their pages. They do, however provide valuable pointers to action and reflection and useful check-lists of important items to consider. The first major attempt to cover all aspects of the development process from the point of view of NGOs was the Oxfam *Field Director's Handbook* (Oxfam 1985).

Supporting Development Action: From Identification to Evaluation, a methodological guide produced by COTA in 1992, is a less ambitious but very user-friendly publication written mainly for NGOs (see Beadoux *et al.* 1992). It is structured to comply with the four commonly understood development action stages in the life of a project—identification, programming, monitoring and evaluation—and contains a very useful bibliography, including material in French which is not commonly referred to in the English speaking world. The authors stress that the methodologies described should be adopted flexibly as an illustrated checklist.

The *Workbook* published by AGKED and MISEREOR provides a comprehensive coverage of evaluation methods and includes the following case studies: the GRAAP method of animation (Groupe de Recherche et d'Appui pour l'Autopromotion Paysanne); target-oriented project planning (ZOPP); development education and leadership training for action (DELTA); and the ENDA-GRAF (Group Recherche Action Formation) group approach (ENDA is an international NGO); and an annotated bibliography which includes German experience. It concentrates on the search for a systematic methodology and precise instruments which are seen as necessary for a validated evaluation. This is seen within the context of cost-minimisation and an attempt to gain a consistency between the financial input needed for evaluation and the usefulness of its findings.

The crux of this methodology is to be found in the partnership of supporting and implementing agencies. Opposed to the investigative function of conventional evaluations the preference here is to utilise evaluation as an instrument of dialogue and learning and therefore an integral component of cooperation. Subsequently, evaluation is on a joint basis and procedures are determined as such. Terms of reference (TOR) are drawn up in the spirit of cooperation through a process of dialogue and negotiation; the final version being based on consensus and serving as the key reference document for the evaluation. The TOR are then translated into operational questions that are prioritised. For each of these an approach is established by which the necessary information is to be ascertained. Thus:

> The TOR cannot be restricted—as often happens in practice—to the
> formulation of questions while leaving it to the evaluation team to
> find the methods how to answer these questions. (AGKED and
> MISEREOR 1991:27)

The TOR therefore include the methodology to be used to elicit the qualitative and quantitative information necessary for the evaluation. This 'methodical openness' is seen as essential in gaining trust between partners and participants in the evaluation process. The methods and instruments themselves must be adaptable and oriented towards the socio-cultural context and specifics of the project conditions. The evaluation process's search for 'validity, reliability, and representability' is rendered culturally relevant.

Yet despite this willingness to incorporate some of the participatory methods as defined and developed through the use of the localised knowledge of the partner organisation, *The Workbook* rejects full participatory methods. Viewed as useful only where democratisation and the necessary knowledge and experience of participants is available, extended participation is seen as a hindrance in all but a few project evaluations. These methods are criticised as being determined by the learning and action processes of the participants, and for failing to take account of the procedures involved in project funding, without really questioning those procedures. Furthermore:

> Through new levels of awareness reached and gained in social
> action/reflection, objectives and measures/practices may be changed
> in a way which was not part of the original project application. As a
> result, it may become increasingly difficult for the participants of such
> an evaluation to arrange the contents and findings of their analysis in

such a way that changes, achievements etc. can at least partly be attributed to the project/programme in its original form. (AGKED and MISEREOR 1991:38)

One has to ask which is the more important, social development itself, or the evaluation of it? In this sense evaluation merely serves the purpose of reinforcing NGO preoccupation with the concept of 'the project'. It is in danger of ignoring the wider issues of development and of who has power and control over resources. Stephen (1991) has referred to this as 'the project trap' and has expressed a need to look at development on a more long term and macro basis, ignoring the tradition of discrete project phases if true social development is to be achieved.

Insiders and Outsiders

In a recent discussion paper from the World Bank, Uphoff (1992) takes up the distinction between 'emic' and 'etic' approaches elaborated earlier by anthropologists and linguists. He thereby brings into focus the central issue of 'insiders' and 'outsiders', and draws a distinction between so-called 'objective' knowledge derived through 'neutral' information collection and analysis, and the 'subjective' knowledge of 'insiders' which has often been regarded as inferior because of its biased nature. He elaborates methodologies which can be used for more local level involvement in appraisal monitoring and evaluation, which bring together work undertaken at Cornell over the past few years (see also Uphoff 1986).

The principle of objective, scientifically validated knowledge assumes that eventually a more complete understanding will allow the development of more workable systems. It implicitly underpins efforts at social engineering which aim to change existing cultures and institutions within the beneficiary societies into forms which will make them more conducive to the development effort (and more compliant to external manipulation?).

While no evaluation would be complete without taking into account both 'emic' and 'etic' perspectives and utilising both quantitative and qualitative information, there has been a tendency until relatively recently to down play 'insider' knowledge. With the rise of interest in indigenous knowledge (see Richards 1985, and Brokensha, Warren and Werner 1980) and in 'putting the poor first' (see Chambers et al. 1989), there has however been a shift not just to include the beneficiaries in the evaluation of development projects but also to see their participation as one of the key ways in which more effective projects and programmes can be designed and implemented. By including the poor more centrally, there is an expectation that this will generate more responsibility for maintaining something that they feel is their own.

A potential problem with the distinction between 'emic' and 'etic' perspectives is that it is too simplistic. There are many sorts of outsiders and their are inevitably conflicts of interest within beneficiary communities. Who decides what insider knowledge is? Is insider knowledge not also that privileged knowledge which secures advantages (as in insider trading).

From RRA to PRA

It was Robert Chambers who stated there was a, 'need (for) information that (was) relevant, timely, accurate and usable' (Cernea 1985:399). Existing systems of data/information collection were not only inaccurate but costly. 'Rural development tourism', with its anti-poverty bias, as well as large scale sociological and anthropological studies were both deemed inadequate for the more focused 'grassroots development' of the eighties.

Based on optimal ignorance ('what isn't worth knowing') and appropriate imprecision ('the degree of accuracy that is unnecessary') this methodology could establish what needed to be known. Furthermore it could do so in a time efficient and cost effective manner thereby providing an 'optimal trade-off' between the traditional methods of data collection. The fact that RRA has not actually been carefully defined, other than as 'organised commonsense', 'eclectic', 'versatile' and 'inventive' (Cernea 1985:410–11) has allowed it to absorb much of the new data/information collection techniques. This is no more apparent than in RRA Notes as published by the International Institute for Environment and Development (IIED). With articles concerning 'participatory rural appraisal' (PRA), 'participatory learning methods' (PALM), 'rapid assessment procedures' (RAP), 'rapid rural systems analysis' (RRSA), and 'agroecosystem analysis' (AEA), it is clear just how all embracing RRA has now become.

Over a period of seven years these notes have documented the changes that have taken place in RRA as perceived and initiated by the practitioners themselves. For development practitioners and academics alike they provide a lively insight into the trials and tribulations of those at the forefront of appraisal, monitoring, and evaluation. By far the most comprehensive coverage of the techniques and methodologies used in RRA are provided by RRA Notes numbers 7 and 13, both proceedings from RRA workshops held in Sussex and Bangalore, respectively. By refusing to limit the Notes to articles purely concerning fieldwork, interesting pieces on a variety of themes have been contributed. Of particular interest has been the ongoing debate over the role of the 'outsider' (Fussel No. 9, Scheuermeier No. 10, Messerschmidt No. 12, and Johnson No. 12); the need for training to promote attitudinal change (Cromwell No. 9, Mitchell and Slim Nos 9 and 10, and Overview No. 11), and the use of RRA for assessing women's needs in traditionally patriarchal communities (Grady et al. No. 10 and Hosain No. 12). More recently the Notes have been dedicated to in-depth discussions on specific issues including participatory learning methods and analysis, wealth ranking and applications for health.

The dynamics of RRA have allowed it to elude professionalisation and agency capture despite the constant danger of it becoming the new orthodoxy. The perpetual state of flux that it appears to be in, continually adapting to changing conditions in the field, is made apparent by the contributions of the *RRA Notes* readership. As techniques, and those employing them, have proliferated, the procedure has become more and more guided by the respondents themselves. By providing a forum by which practitioners of RRA can share ideas, these notes have managed to chart how RRA has evolved from a method of extracting information in a time efficient and cost effective manner, into participatory rural appraisal (PRA) and a method for the promotion of local capacity building and empowerment. This change in emphasis suggests that PRA may well have severed its links with the conventional paradigm that RRA appeared to be based on. It may be more akin to the more radical evaluation approaches outlined later, but as yet there is very little within the literature to suggest that the evaluator has entirely relinquished his/her control over the process of information collection, and more importantly, its dissemination. Nevertheless it is important to recognise the potential of PRA to address this issue of the decentralisation of knowledge and thereby of power.

In the United States, the work of the Programme for International Development at Clark University, has paralleled that of RRA in Britain with work in Kenya and more recently with ActionAid in The Gambia. An increasing number of Northern and Southern NGOs such as Oxfam (see Neefjes 1992), are utilising participatory appraisal methods in developing their relationships with client groups. Many of these initiatives are identified in *RRA Notes*.

From Collection to Collective Production

From the middle of the 1980s, rapid rural appraisal was undergoing a change. The literature began to emphasise participatory rural appraisal as the focus shifted from rapid collection of information towards the building of consensus over shared values and directions, the pooling of information and discussions about what it is appropriate to know. There was a growing recognition of the 'value-pluralism' that surrounded development initiatives.

Methodologies employed involved learning people's priorities, identifying intangible benefits and the elaboration of ways and means whereby beneficiaries might be more centrally incorporated into the design and implementation of development projects (details of the different methodologies being developed can be found in Chapter 5 of this volume and in Pratt and Loizos 1993 as well as in editions of *RRA Notes*). They include such things as auto- and self-evaluation, farmer to farmer extension, focused group discussions, ZOPP techniques and the development of logical frameworks (see Coleman, IIED *RRA Notes*, IIED/IDS 1992). The emphasis on time cutting seems to have diminished as more attention is devoted to enhancing constructive involvement or participation, between donors and recipients, mediated by a proliferation of quasi-independent NGOs with a remit for the continuous collection and processing of information and discussion of direction in a continuously changing environment.

Time frames for implementation seem to be being redrawn as development workers recognise the often lengthy nature of the processes they are embarking on. Beneficiaries are not just consulted in the design of indicators for the measurement of achievement but are seen as the prime evolvers of such indicators. The parameters that once separated evaluation from appraisal and from monitoring within the project cycle are being increasingly blurred. The ways in which information is being collected, the uses to which it is being put, are seen in some instances as more important than the scientific validity of such information.

In the autumn of 1992, the IIED in cooperation with the Institute of Development Studies held a workshop with the aim of bringing together the results of the *Beyond Farmer First* programme of research support and institutional collaboration. A large number of papers were commissioned and three very useful overview papers presented. The first examined and synthesised some of the major themes surrounding the analysis of rural people's knowledge for agricultural research, extension and community based development. A second overview paper examined the implications for methodologies of changing theory for development work. A third overview paper explored the changes in institutional arrangements that appear to be taking place to put decentralised and participatory approaches and methods on the central agendas of research institutions and those concerned with agricultural research and development. The workshop dealt with a whole variety of different perspectives, not confined merely to agricultural extension and research.

Radical Alternatives and the Rights to Measure Value

Accused of ignoring the dynamics of sociopolitical change by failing to involve fully its participants, methods of 'cost-effective' evaluation of social development have been much criticised. There have been calls for a more radical perspective that perceives participation to be an end in itself; and participatory evaluation as the means of achieving it. Evaluation is a form of enquiry where the end is information. Information is power and evaluation is powerful (cited in *Search News*, April/June 1991:7).

This form of evaluation has evolved from the perceived failure of three decades of development to address the issues of poverty alleviation and basic needs. Consequently, the role of 'experts' has come under close scrutiny. Their reliance on impersonal, universal and objective knowledge has been transcended as the need for more personal, localised and subjective knowledge has become essential for more appropriate development interventions.

It is a process more akin to methods of monitoring such as that of 'self-evaluation' or 'ongoing evaluation'. These methods have a long history but have been undermined because of the perception that they are subjective and do not provide genuine evaluations. This problem is exemplified in Roche's 'Case Study of an Evaluation in Mali' where concern is expressed over the donor's faith in the authenticity of the external evaluation due to its reliance on a process of auto-evaluation for indicators and information. This can be seen as a consequence of the relationship between the donor or implementing agency and the beneficiaries; what Tendler (1982) has referred to as 'enlightened top-down'.

Yet in this model methods of participatory evaluation no longer adopt the characteristics of information sharing and consultation but take on more dynamic features enabling beneficiaries to partake in decision making and initiate action. By accepting the validity of different perspectives, both cultural and personal, the relationships between agents of change and beneficiaries are altered. Banuri (1990) provides a comprehensive account of how these changes have evolved. More importantly he suggests that the future no longer lies in further adapting modernisation theory so that it better suits the cultural needs of 'target groups' as the positivist paradigm would suggest. What is in fact required is the outright rejection of modernisation theory and the positing of alternatives.

In order for the improvement in welfare of Third World people to become possible we have to stop believing that this is only something 'we' can do for 'them'; we have to stop trying to quantify and measure the 'quality of life' (or other indicators of 'development') because these measurements become a licence to intervene in 'their'lives on the grounds that 'we' know what is objectively and undoubtedly good for them (Marglin 1990:66).

This model argues that the realisation that beneficiaries have something to offer to the process of development is insufficient; what is more important is the realisation that the beliefs and views that they do offer are at least as valid as any so-called expert's. Furthermore their expression represents a community's unequivocal right to self-determination and is a prerequisite for appropriate, and therefore, sustainable development. Through this process, which involves the decentralisation of knowledge and the recognition of the existence of relative sets of values, true social development can occur; social development that has its foundations firmly rooted in participatory evaluation.

If the right to define welfare and progress were to be unconditionally restored to indigenous people it is true that they would make mistakes, just as the development profession has made mistakes. But, unlike the latter, they would learn from their mistakes and they will adjust their behaviour (Marglin 1990:66).

Fourth Generation Evaluation

It is 'fourth generation evaluation' that presents the most challenging case for a totally new approach to evaluation and does so, ironically, in a scientific manner. This fact that does not go amiss with its authors who state that, 'it is only for purposes of exposition that we lay them (the responsibilities of the fourth generation evaluator) out in what appears to be a linear format' (Guba and Lincoln 1989:72).

This is an ambitious work, and the authors declare their intention, 'to define an emergent but mature approach to evaluation that moves beyond science—not just getting to the 'facts'—to include the myriad human, political, social, cultural and contextual elements that are involved' (1989:8). It provides a thought provoking challenge to future thinking. By systematically discrediting the assumptions on which the scientific/positivist paradigm is built, Guba and Lincoln reiterate Banuri and present a well argued, if sometime abstract case for an alternative. But this book is not just a critique of conventional scientific methods; it provides an alternative 'responsive constructivist evaluation.'

This new approach is based on two key elements: responsive focusing and constructivist methodology. It is responsive focusing that allows the boundaries of the evaluation to be set by the constructions and interactions of its stakeholders. A constructivist methodology provides the wider framework in which 'truth' and 'fact' are recognised for their subjectivity. The positivist paradigm and the belief system it is based on are rejected.

What emerges from this process are not conclusions or recommendations based on 'objective' value judgements but an 'agenda for negotiation' based on the claims, concerns and issues that were not resolved during the dialogue that is the evaluation process. In this format evaluation creates a forum for debate and its findings, having emanated from the stakeholders themselves, become impossible to ignore. The dialogue that this process initiates is sustained as the stakeholders seek to create more informed and sophisticated constructions. Consequently, 'evaluations are never complete but are suspended for logistical reasons such as timing of a mandated decision or because resources are exhausted' (Guba and Lincoln 1989:42).

But the adoption of such a radical approach depends on two important switches. The first Guba and Lincoln claim is the easier and merely requires the evaluator to allow the stakeholders' claims, concerns and issues to provide the salient points for the evaluation. The second, and harder switch, calls for the outright rejection of the conventional scientific paradigm and its endless search for 'truth': endless, because truth, as the constructivist paradigm recognises, is subjective. Adopting this second switch allows for a plurality of knowledge to emerge. With such a process at work generalisations become redundant. Evaluations become time and context bound with relevance only to those involved since, 'the world is brought into being by the participation of those who participate' (Guba and Lincoln 1989:100).

In their final analysis Guba and Lincoln offer no solutions or formulae for evaluation. They realise that to do so would render evaluation ineffective by its universality. More importantly, by providing a 'blueprint' the process would lose its dynamic and become subject to control. This result has become all too familiar as evaluators have increasingly chosen to allow for responsive focusing whilst maintaining the framework of the conventional scientific paradigm. Subsequently the evaluator becomes an investigator seeking to discover which of the stakeholders' perspectives is nearer to 'reality'. Thus the control over the proceedings are relinquished but the final analysis remains firmly in the domain of the evaluators and their sponsors.

Participatory Evaluation

The result of these changes has been to focus more on 'participatory evaluation' which goes beyond the mere involvement of beneficiaries in some externally conceived intervention. It calls for an alternative approach not only to evaluation but also to the dominant modernisation paradigm. It is an approach that finds its roots in the failure of the development effort to significantly improve the standard of living of all but a few in the so called 'Third World', and to circumvent the many barriers that prevent the effective and efficient disbursement of resources to those most in need. The result has been a call for people to define and take greater responsibility for their own development, on their own terms, and pursue it in their own way. 'Participatory evaluation' becomes not only the means by which to create the dialogue necessary for such a process to develop but an integral part of the process itself.

Participatory evaluation methodologies are elaborated on the basis of a rather different set of premises and thus values. Guba and Lincoln outline the most important of these (see Box 2.1 below).

Box 2.1

* 'Truth' is a matter of consensus among informed and sophisticated constructors, not of correspondence with an objective reality.

* 'Facts' have no meaning except within some value framework; hence there cannot be an 'objective' assessment of any proposition.

* 'Causes' and 'effects' do not exist except by imputation; hence accountability is a relative matter and implicates all interacting parties (entities) equally.

* Phenomena can be understood only within the context in which they are studied; findings from one context cannot be generalised to another; neither problems, nor their solutions can be generalised from one setting to another.

* Interventions are not stable; when they are introduced into a particular context they will be at least as much affected (changed) by that context as they are likely to affect the context.

* Change cannot be engineered; it is a nonlinear process that involves the introduction of new information, and increased sophistication in its use, into the constructions of the involved humans.

* Evaluation produces data in which facts and values are inextricably linked. Valuing is an essential part of the evaluation process, providing the basis for an attributed meaning.

* Accountability is a characteristic of a conglomerate of mutual and simultaneous shapers, no one of which nor one subset of which can be uniquely singled out for praise or blame.

* Evaluators are subjective partners with stakeholders in the literal creation of data.

* Evaluators are orchestrators of a negotiation process that attempts to culminate in consensus on better informed and more sophisticated constructions.

* Evaluation data derived from constructivist inquiry have neither special status nor legitimation; they represent simply another construction to be taken into account in the move toward consensus.

Guba and Lincoln (1989:44-45)

Richards (1985), in an evaluation of a UNICEF project in Chile, offers a more narrative account of an evaluation, but reiterates Guba and Lincoln's views that, 'whatever else evaluation is, it is communication. It is a form of communication because an evaluation sends messages from somebody to somebody' (Richards 1985:2). Therefore the focus remains on the issue that whoever controls the processes by which these 'messages' are disseminated controls the messages themselves. His rather refreshing and satirical account combines both practice and theory in an attempt to create a vivid picture of, what he terms 'illuminative evaluation'. Once again the conventional paradigm and its associated cost effective and systems approach is rejected in favour of a more participatory based study.

The systems approach is itself a set of ideas and forces, as such it is a weapon used to strengthen a certain culture. By and large it is a weapon used by the managerial elite to serve its own interest (Richards 1985:209).

Responsible for denying legitimacy to other cultures that fail to use its terminology, Richards considers the positivist paradigm to be 'an instrument of domination' (1985:208). Consequently great emphasis is placed on the use of participants' language . They are seen to be the experts and their contribution to the evaluation, as those at the heart of the programme, is indispensable . They are thereby given priority in an attempt to learn about the processes involved in cultural and attitudinal change.

Like fourth generation evaluation, participants are allowed to shape the process and reach consensus through inter-action via a system of 'progressive focusing'. By quoting interviews and providing concrete examples in the final report, what is communicated becomes a vivid picture, creating empathy amongst its readers. Through a system of triangulation these accounts are then checked and quantified thereby improving the accuracy of the whole process. Hence 'illuminatory evaluation makes its subject stand in the light and be visible' (1985:2), not hide behind a smokescreen of methodological ritual and 'objectivity'.

A study of Richards's account invites theoretical and methodological debate. Not only does Richards reject the 'objectivity' of evaluators but the scholarly writings that surround them. His work is revolutionary not only in the empowering approach that he suggests can take place though the evaluation but in the way that he suggests it. His book is a personal account. With humour and with passion he makes the reader aware of the moral dilemmas that every evaluator should face in his or her work.

Patton's book *Creative Evaluation* (1987) can be seen as furthering the discussions in the *RRA Notes*, stressing the importance of the individual skills and attitudinal characteristics of the evaluator. Here great emphasis is placed on the importance of the evaluator as a catalyst of change. It is a book rivalled only by Feuerstein's 'Partners in Evaluation' in terms of its amicable style. Written in the first person singular and using mostly personal anecdotal evidence Quinn Patton, as an evaluator himself, emphasises the importance and vocational aspects of evaluating. Despite being based on the same theoretical framework (i.e. the rejection of the conventional paradigm) as Richards, and Guba and Lincoln, one cannot help but feel that he over emphasises the role of the evaluator. The almost messianic depiction of the evaluator is delivered as if it were the sermon of a religious convert. It lacks the subtlety of either Guba and Lincoln or Richards but nevertheless in its own way presents some very important issues to be considered in the search for an alternative approach to evaluation.

The evaluator must be aware of the patterns of socialisation and professionalisation that constrain what are perceived to be discretionary judgements. Once realised the evaluator becomes emancipated, free to be loyal to a situation rather than a model or paradigm.

Creative evaluators are active-reactive-adaptive in working with decision makers, information users and stakeholders to focus the evaluation on meaningful, appropriate and researchable questions the answers to which will be useful for programme improvement and decision making (Patton 1987:59).

Creativity becomes an attitude, a realisation that the status quo is not necessarily the most effective means by which to proceed. It thereby becomes a necessary condition for effective evaluation. But it is not sufficient as Patton would have us believe; participatory evaluation is far too much an interactive and dynamic process to solely depend on the evaluator. What the evaluator can bring to the process is a different outlook and, therefore, a willingness to serve as a medium between stakeholders. Creative evaluation allows for a particularly responsive medium that via adaptive techniques and a flexible methodology can assist beneficiaries in finding their own solutions to their own problems. This book not only provides the means by which the evaluator can become involved in the theoretical debate over alternative participatory approaches to evaluation but also some of the means with which to implement these alternatives. It is here that Patton surpasses his fellow colleagues of participatory evaluation. By supplying an extensive selection of techniques whilst acknowledging the limitations of such a selection, he provides the reader with far more information than just a theoretical framework or a particular case study.

Furthermore great emphasis is given to the role of the evaluator to instigate change in all those involved in the evaluation process. As a convert it is the evaluator's mission to save all who he or she might meet. Hence, 'situationally responsive and active-reactive-adaptive evaluators will find opportunities in virtually any evaluation to train decision makers, funders, information users, staff, and stakeholders of all kinds in the basics of evaluation' (Patton 1987:250).

Most importantly it stresses the need for asset analysis as opposed to an assessment of needs. Creative evaluation should concentrate on the strengths and assets of its stakeholders and not belittle them implicitly by emphasising their weaknesses. By emphasising this change in perspective, Patton identifies an important role for evaluation in the process of social development. Evaluation becomes a process by which attributes can be identified and developed rather than deficiencies corrected. It no longer concentrates on the differences between stakeholders and seeks to change them; rather it concentrates on differences in an attempt to understand them. By doing so it creates a forum for discussion; 'an agenda for negotiation'. Thus, participatory evaluation fulfils its facilitative function, rejecting conventional evaluation and its potential to manipulate. The proponents of such a process, as reviewed in this section, do not see evaluation as distinct from social development but an integral part of its evolution and consolidation.

CHAPTER THREE

CASE STUDIES IN THE EVALUATION
OF SOCIAL DEVELOPMENT

3.1 EVALUATING SOCIAL DEVELOPMENT: A CASE STUDY OF THE CATHOLIC DEVELOPMENT COMMISSION, ZIMBABWE

Veronica Brand and Cosmas Wakatama
The Catholic Development Commission, Zimbabwe

Introduction
The Catholic Development Commission was established in 1972 by the Zimbabwe Catholic Bishops' Conference to carry out the social work of the church. At the time of its formation it was known as the Commission on Social Service and Development. However, after its first major evaluation, the name was changed in 1984 to the Catholic Development Commission (CADEC), due to a shift in the emphasis of its work from social welfare to development. The Commission implements its work through a national office and six diocesan offices. At the national level the policy and decision making body is the National Executive Committee composed of the President who is a Bishop, the Diocesan Development Coordinators, the Diocesan Bishop's Appointees (in all cases religious) who oversee the work of the diocesan office, the National Chairman (who up to date has been a lay person), the national office staff, and the elected chairpersons of diocesan committees. Over the years the Commission has established partnerships with different Church-related agencies overseas which have enabled the Commission to implement its development activities.

In each diocese there is a similar body, i.e. the diocesan committee, composed of the Bishop, his appointee (Ex-Officio), the Diocesan Coordinators, members of the diocesan field teams and elected representatives from the communities with whom the Commission is working in development programmes and projects. As each diocese is autonomous, further diocesan structures vary from diocese to diocese. In some dioceses below the diocesan committees there are district and area committees and in other dioceses there are deanery and parish committees.

One of the functions of each diocesan committee is to assess and approve project applications from different communities.

The two Papal Encyclicals, the *'Development of Peoples' (Populorum Progressio* by Pope Paul VI, 1967) and *'Social Concern' (Sollicitudo Rei Socialis* by Pope John Paul II, 1987) could be described as providing the charter for the Commission's work. The Commission's work is devoted primarily to the promotion and development of the whole person. As man/woman is both the subject and vehicle of his/her own development, this necessitates a specific type of methodology in the Commission's work. This approach aims at:

• creating awareness in the people of their own life situations and its problems and of their own abilities and potentialities;

• motivating people to change their life situations ;

• involving people fully, through maximum participation at all stages in implementing this change;

• assisting them to acquire the necessary and appropriate knowledge and skills;

• giving them confidence and vision to see life as a process of change which is oriented to the ultimate goal of self-reliance.

Because of its chosen approach to development work, the Commission sees the development education programme as the cornerstone of its work. The development education programme has two major components, (i) 'awareness creation' and (ii) 'training aimed at empowering people to fully participate in their own development'. Through the process of awareness creation, communities are assisted in identifying their needs and problems and encouraged to move from complaining about these towards some action aimed at solving the problems or responding to the needs.

The action decided upon usually takes the form of a community or group project. The type and extent of the programme differ from community to community and from diocese to diocese. However, most of the dioceses are involved in the following programmes: agriculture and savings clubs; water development and garden projects; adult literacy; primary health care; AIDS; micro-project programmes which are small-scale, community based projects; nutrition and pre-school care; sanitation; income-generating projects; and training.

Within each programme there exists the possibility of projects. For example, the agriculture programme would include such projects as agricultural cooperatives, community vegetable gardens, agriculture inputs, store-rooms, savings clubs, training, and small scale livestock breeding projects. Projects must meet the following conditions to be approved by CADEC: they must involve and serve a community and not just an individual; the project must arise from the real needs of the whole community; the community must participate at every stage of the project; and the community must contribute to the project, whether in labour or locally available resources and skills.

Preparation of the Evaluation

The decision in late 1989 to undertake a second major evaluation was not imposed from outside but was actually taken by the Commission itself. This need was recognised by both the Commission and by its overseas church partners, who over the years have continued to collaborate in sponsoring the Commission's structures and programmes. Because of this long-standing collaboration, the Commission also decided to involve its partners at every stage by giving them the opportunity to comment or make suggestions based on their experiences from other countries. Five years had passed since the implementation of the recommendations from the last evaluation undertaken by the Commission. Significant shifts had occurred in the Commission's mode and scope of operation as a result of the policy of decentralisation which had been adopted after the last evaluation. As a result, there was a need to review and evaluate the developments that had occurred with a view to providing feedback to enhance the work of the Commission.

Other concerns and questions that prompted the evaluation included: how effective are the Commission's programmes in alleviating the situation of the poor?; do the new structures that have evolved since decentralisation respond to the needs of the communities in the dioceses?; to what extent has the Commission achieved its goal of implementing the social teachings of the Church by providing an integrated approach to social work and pastoral needs?

Consultations on the Objectives

The overall aims of the evaluation exercise were agreed upon by the National Executive in late 1989. In order to convert these broad aims into concrete objectives, several steps were taken. First, the main resource person began the task of familiarisation with the work of CADEC. This involved a thorough study of all the written documentation held at national level, including the Minutes of Executive meetings, Diocesan Three Year Plans and Annual Reports (National and Diocesan) in order to identify some of the key issues and questions. Informal discussions held with National Office staff also highlighted some of the key originating questions that were being asked.

A list was then made of the key questions and issues that seemed to be recurring. After reflection by the national team, a preliminary list of objectives was formulated and circulated to the diocesan offices for comment. A suggested outline for a possible participative process involving the diocesan committee members was then drawn up by the resource person. Each diocese selected its own method of involving the committee members in a participative way in the re-formulation of objectives. Some chose the workshop technique, others discussed each objective in the context of a formal meeting. In all cases, an attempt was made to identify the following:

(i) Which of the suggested objectives were pertinent? Which should be changed?

(ii) Were there any other objectives not included that should be added?

Draft terms of reference were then drawn up by the national team, taking into account the feedback already received from the diocesan committees. A special meeting was also attended by representatives of the main overseas partner agencies, CEBEMO and MISEREOR. Adjustments were made to the objectives and the overall terms of reference, incorporating the feedback received from the diocesan committees, the members of the Executive and the overseas partner agencies.

Evaluation Objectives
The following were the final objectives agreed upon:

(i) To assess the achievements, shortcomings, and hence the efficiency of the planning and implementation of CADEC national and diocesan development programmes in the light of the decentralisation that took place between 1985 and 1989.

(ii) To assess the effectiveness of CADEC diocesan development programmes in responding to the needs of the poor and promoting self-reliance.

(iii) To determine how far the diocesan and national training programmes complement one another.

(iv) To assess effectiveness of both the diocesan and national training programmes in increasing the people's participation in their own development.

(v) To identify the advantages and disadvantages of decentralised funding of diocesan projects and programmes since 1985.

(vi) To assess the extent to which efforts made since 1985 to promote self-reliance within CADEC have been successful.

(vii) To assess the extent to which beneficiaries have participated in the identification, implementation and evaluation of diocesan projects.

(viii) To assess the effectiveness of the Commission's national structures (i.e. the General Assembly, the National Executive, the National Office) in responding to: (a) the needs of the CADEC diocesan offices; (b) the needs of the communities served by the diocesan offices.

(ix) To assess the effectiveness of the CADEC diocesan structures in implementing the programmes of the Commission.

(x) To ascertain the degree of awareness regarding the role and functions of CADEC and the image of CADEC held by: (a) local church personnel, (b) local community members and (c) project beneficiaries.

(xi) To determine if there are other needs identified by these groups that fall within CADEC's terms of reference but which are not covered by existing CADEC programmes.

(xii) To assess the extent to which CADEC has been able to integrate the social and pastoral work of the church in the implementation of its programmes.

Although there was a substantial amount of information available about the organisation and its activities over the last five years, there was nowhere where the vision statement and the objectives of the Commission were clearly stated. The information that was available even from the organisation's terms of reference only pointed to or indicated what should be the objectives of the organisation. Conclusions about the objectives of the Commission had to be drawn from such records as the minutes of the Executive Committee, annual reports of the National Commission and Minutes of the Annual General Meetings. Therefore one could conclude that the base line data at the national level was very inadequate as a starting point for the evaluation. The same applied to individual programmes at diocesan level. It was evident that the records kept at the diocesan level were not very helpful in terms of trying to determine the objectives of each individual programme nor did they contain the statistical information necessary to assess its progress over the years. Very little consistent, comparative and complete information about projects was available by way of baseline information. Although a major evaluation exercise of the Commission's activities and structures had been carried out five years earlier, the findings of this evaluation had not been fully utilised. This was mainly due to the fact that the previous evaluation had been of the traditional 'outsider' type, far removed from the Commission's personnel and the beneficiaries of the different programmes. The majority of the Commission's personnel and the beneficiaries of the programmes had not been directly involved in either the drawing up of these projects or in the data collection and analysis. As a result, they did not identify themselves with the findings.

From the beginning, the participatory evaluation process adopted was expected to operate at two levels–the national level and diocesan level. The close interaction and collaboration between the two levels of implementation, rather than either a 'top-down' dictatorial approach or a separatist approach, was seen as essential. However, this meant that there was a constant tension between the need for the local CADEC structures to identify and determine the nature and process of their own evaluation according to local needs, and the attempt to standardise some areas of the evaluation in order to be able to address key questions relating to the effects of the decentralisation process undertaken seven years previously. Maintaining the delicate balance between the national/local levels continued to be a challenge throughout the evaluation.

Even at the early stages of the evaluation it was evident that there were differences in expectation between dioceses:

- some dioceses had already identified their own terms of reference, had held preliminary workshops to seek feedback from their grass roots members and were anxious to be as autonomous as possible;

- other dioceses had no prior experience of planning an evaluation exercise, and looked to the national team for a detailed 'blue print' to follow.

Bearing in mind the need for a flexible and negotiated dialogue between the national and diocesan levels, a draft work plan and time scale were drawn up by the resource person in consultation with the national team. A meeting of diocesan coordinators with the national team led to the search for consensus about areas that needed to be standardised across dioceses and areas to be left entirely to the discretion of the local (diocesan) level.

The evaluation process was divided into five stages.

Execution Phase

Methodology

The participatory methodology used in the evaluation relied upon the close interaction of evaluation teams operating at national and diocesan level. Diocesan evaluation teams were selected by the CADEC Committee in each diocese, using agreed criteria developed jointly with the national team to ensure representatives and participation. Each team had between 4 to 8 members, including staff, committee members and project beneficiaries, mixed in terms of sex and age, and of sufficient educational background to be able to record accurately. The Diocesan CADEC Coordinator served as a team leader.

The national evaluation team was made up of the National Director, the Development Education Officer, and the main resource person aided by two student research assistants attached to CADEC for 3 months. The role of the national team was to facilitate the overall planing, implementation and coordination of the evaluation exercise, with particular emphasis on the national aspects and on standardised areas. It also interviewed key church figures at diocesan and national level as well as members of the National Executive; it led focused group discussions with diocesan committees and staff and it planned and facilitated both evaluation training workshops, and the final evaluation workshop. The role of the diocesan evaluation team was to plan and implement the field phase of the evaluation. It also took part in both evaluation training workshops (preparing for data gathering and data analysis) and used the field methods identified below.

A wide range of people involved in the work of the Commission participated in the evaluation process. The roles of the various 'actors' in the evaluation could be summarised as follows:

Project Staff. Their participation differed according to their staff position and whether or not they were members of the evaluation team. All the staff participated in group discussions and contributed to the evaluation design at local level.

Diocesan Coordinators / Team Leaders. These generally served as evaluation team leaders. They were actively involved in all five phases of the evaluation: the formulation of objectives; evaluation planning and design; sampling; construction of data collecting instruments; interviewing local partners and church personnel; and planning and supervision of the field phase of evaluation. They were participants in the evaluation training workshops and took responsibility for follow up in the area of data processing and analysis in close liaison with the resource person. Finally, they organised and supervised the analysis of data and the writing of the report and facilitated feedback and discussion of preliminary findings at diocesan level.

Programme Beneficiaries. They participated in group evaluation discussions and group interviews in relation to the affairs of their particular project. In each diocese, some project beneficiaries took part in evaluation workshops organised at local, area or diocesan committee level while a few participated throughout the data gathering phase as members of the diocesan evaluation.

Resource Person. The resource person was responsible for overall coordination of the design and implementation of the evaluation, working in close collaboration with the National Director and Development Education Officer and helped to provide technical resource support through planning, skills training, assistance with developing data collection instruments and aids for data analysis and report writing.

Overseas Partner Agencies. The direct supportive role of the overseas partners was focused at three key points during the evaluation:

(i) *Beginning:* the finalisation of the terms of reference (including the objectives, methodology, and work plan).

(ii) *Middle:* discussion with the national team and contact in the field with one evaluation team during the data-gathering exercise.

(iii) *End:* discussion with the national team and full participation in the final evaluation workshop.

Field Methods
In order to obtain the wide range of information identified as necessary, a variety of field methods were used:

A. *Group Interviews.* 251 project beneficiary groups were interviewed, spread throughout the six dioceses .

B. *Individual Interviews.* A total of 500 project beneficiaries were interviewed. Individual interviews (some structured; some unstructured) were also used with CADEC staff at diocesan and national level; with bishops and church leaders; local partners; diocesan representatives; and former CADEC leaders.

C. *Focused Group Discussions.* These were conducted among diocesan committees, diocesan staff, and national CADEC groups. These were sometimes done in the context of a workshop format.

D. *Archival Research.* Research was undertaken into the records of the National Office, diocesan offices, and project groups.

E. *Observation Techniques.* These were used mainly with project groups, in some instances using prepared observation schedules as aids.

F. *Case Studies.* One or two individual projects were selected in each diocese.

G. *Questionnaires.* These were carried out among members (present and past) of the CADEC National Executive.

H. *Team Assessment Sheets.* These were used among project groups.

Indicators
The evaluation objectives that had been identified fell into two broad categories; namely, efficiency and effectiveness.

Efficiency objectives related to the use of resources: Does the impact of the programme in terms of outcome (the output) justify the amount of resources put into it (the input)? Because of the participatory nature of the evaluation, it was thought inappropriate to attempt a full cost benefit analysis. Instead, an assessment was sought of efficiency at two levels: the use of resources in programme planning and implementation at national and diocesan level; and the use of resources (money, materials, time and training) at project level.

Effectiveness objectives related to the extent to which the programmes and structures of the Commission achieved what they had set out to do. Analysis of these evaluation objectives led to the identification of seven main criteria against which the effectiveness of CADEC structures and programmes were to be judged. These were:

- responding to felt needs;

- promoting self-reliance;

- increasing participation;

- building awareness;

• integrating social and pastoral work of the church;

• benefitting the poor;

• achieving objectives.

The participation of the diocesan coordinators was sought in identifying the different field methods and the specific indicators against which 'effectiveness' and 'efficiency' could be measured. The schema below proved helpful in working through this process.

Table 3.1

STANDARDS	WHAT are the criteria we use to judge?
EVIDENCE	WHAT information do we need?
SOURCES	WHO has the information? WHERE do we get it?
METHODS	HOW do we get it?

To illustrate the types of indicators that were selected in order to operationalise the various criteria of programme effectiveness, two examples are given below. In each case reference is made to the field methods used to assess the extent to which a given criterion was met (the letters used below to indicate field methods relate to the above list).

Criterion: Promoting Self-reliance

INDICATORS	METHOD
Level and type of local contribution in relation to assistance given by CADEC	A, D
Loan repayment	A, D
Reliance on own resources *vis á vis* dependence on outside resources in solving present problems and making future plans	A, H
Use of profit from income generation projects	A, D

Statements revealing group members' image of CADEC   A, B

Suggestions for changes in CADEC's way of working   A, B

Criterion: Participation

INDICATORS	METHOD
Who initiated the project (members/outsiders)	A, D
Time invested by members in project activity, such as meetings and training etc.	B, D
Type of committee structure	A, E
How long has the Chairperson held office	A, D
Who makes what decisions	A, E
Level of knowledge of group affairs (ordinary member as compared with the group leader)	B
How groups solve the problems they experience	A, B, E

Qualitative and Quantitative Aspects

The balance between qualitative and quantitative aspects of the evaluation was negotiated throughout the process of evaluation planning, preparation and design. Structured data collection instruments were generally used in order to explore the more quantitative aspects, as they provided a basis for comparative analysis. Three examples given below indicate some of the ways in which this was attempted.

(i) In an attempt to measure one dimension of participation, a series of ten simple, fixed, alternative questions was designed to measure group members' knowledge of group affairs. These were asked as part of the individual interviews conducted with the group leader and one ordinary member of the group. This made it possible to calculate a 'participation score', with one point being given for each time the answers given were the same (minimum = 0; maximum = 10). Agreement in the answers given between the group leader and an ordinary group member suggested good information flow and a high level of participation. Comparison of the participation scores of different types of project groups nationally enabled certain important conclusions to be reached.

(ii) One of the evaluation objectives sought to ascertain the awareness that the programme beneficiaries' had of the role and functions of the Commission, and their image of CADEC. This essentially qualitative aspect was explored through the use of a series of seven pairs of code pictures drawn by an artist attached to the literacy programme in one diocese. The pictures attempted to highlight contrasting images of CADEC. Groups were asked to discuss which one of each pair of pictures better expressed what CADEC meant to them. In addition to noting which picture was selected by the group, evaluation team members later analysed the comments made in the context of the group discussion in order to identify key elements of the 'image' of CADEC held by different groups. Because this essentially qualitative technique was used by all diocesan evaluation teams, some important conclusions were able to be reached at national level, based on quantitative analysis of the varying percentages of different types of groups that stressed a given aspect.

(iii) After visiting each project group, evaluation teams were encouraged to sit down together to share their impressions of group performance on each of the seven criteria of effectiveness and on the group efficiency in the use of resources. Teams then filled in an assessment sheet for each project group visited, using a simple 5 point scale indicating the extent to which they felt that each of the criteria of effectiveness and efficiency was met (these scale points were: to a great extent; to some extent; fair, poor; not at all). When teams met later for the workshop on data analysis, use of a scoring technique enabled teams to:

- chart a visual profile of all 251 groups in terms of their overall performance on effectiveness and efficiency criteria;

- compare teams' subjective assessment with the objective assessment of performance in relation to given criteria and;

- analyse common strengths and weaknesses in terms of effectiveness and efficiency of both development programme and diocese.

Interpretation of Data
Interpretation of data during the evaluation process was done at a number of levels:

- by the client group/beneficiaries during the group interviews /discussions held during the field phase of the evaluation;

- by the diocesan evaluation teams throughout the exercise, assisted by the resource person where requested;

- between evaluation teams during the data analysis workshop;

- by project staff in the preparation of diocesan reports;

- by the national team using the collated, computerised data on the standardised aspects of the evaluation;

- by the resource person in sharing feedback with the diocesan evaluation teams during the data analysis and report writing phase;

- by diocesan committee members in their discussions of the draft diocesan reports;

- by all participants in the final evaluation workshop.

The commitment to a participatory methodology made it important to ensure that the analysis and interpretation of findings was not merely a technical activity done by 'outsiders' and fed back to 'insiders', but was instead an important and integral dimension of the evaluation in which all the 'actors' had an opportunity to participate. Reflection and interpretation of team experiences during the field phase was also seen as vitally important to the whole evaluation process.

Reporting Phase

Preparation of evaluation reports was done in two phases at both diocesan and national levels. To ensure that the reporting process itself was participative, a 'bottom up' approach was adopted. Diocesan reports were finalised by local teams before the national report was drafted. Draft reports were then 'tested' with feedback being incorporated into the final reports.

Although diocesan teams worked individually in preparing their diocesan reports, some interaction between the six teams and some 'mutual feedback' was built into the second evaluation training workshop on data analysis and report writing. Teams were grouped regionally in pairs for this workshop, which included the sharing of their experience of the evaluation process and what they had learnt through it, reflection on their major findings, as well as 'hands on' experience in processing and analysing their own data. The combined report of the three regional workshops summarised the major feedback from all six teams, highlighting areas of similarity and difference in their experience and observations. This report became one of the resources available to diocesan teams in preparing their own evaluation reports.

Each diocesan CADEC evaluation team, led by the coordinator/team leader, wrote its own evaluation report covering the evaluation objectives that related to the diocesan level. In some dioceses the actual report writing process involved all members of the team; in others, after preliminary discussion and analysis involving all team members, one or two members worked closely with the team Leader to prepare the evaluation report. Draft evaluation reports were then shared with key people at diocesan level (the bishop, his diocesan appointee, and the CADEC committee) and with the resource person and director at national level. Most dioceses organised a committee meeting to discuss the draft report findings and conclusions. Feedback received on the draft report from local and national level was then incorporated into the revised final diocesan evaluation report. The scope, depth and style of the diocesan evaluation reports differed greatly, according to the particular circumstances of the diocese, the skills of the report writers, the issues arising in the course of the evaluation, and the local CADEC structures in the diocese. Differences between dioceses were also apparent in the ways in which the evaluation findings were disseminated and shared. Most dioceses organised one or more committee meetings to familiarise members with the evaluation findings and to receive their feedback. Those with district, area or parish CADEC structures used these to organise feedback sessions and workshops.

The resource person was tasked with the writing of the final evaluation report. This was intended firstly to address all the objectives of the evaluation, some of which pertained specifically to the national level and were not dealt with in the diocesan reports (e.g. national programmes and national structures). Secondly, the national report addressed overall areas of similarity and difference between dioceses.

The draft national report was developed in light of five main sources of information and analysis:

• diocesan evaluation reports;

• workshops, interviews and documentary analysis undertaken by the national team;

• data compiled from structured interviews with beneficiaries (both groups and individuals). This data was coded at the diocesan level and then fed into the computer at the national level to facilitate analysis;

• direct field experience of national team members gained by contact and monitoring visits to local evaluation teams during data gathering phase;

• sharing and feedback obtained during the three workshops on data analysis and report writing held at regional level.

Final Evaluation Workshop

The three-day final evaluation workshop provided the major forum for processing feedback from the evaluation teams, project managers (i.e. staff and committee members) and overseas partner organisations. The workshop was planned and facilitated jointly by the National Director and resource person, and run by a steering committee which included a representative of the overseas partner agencies. Key conclusions and recommendations from the diocesan reports and the national report were presented and feedback sought from the workshop participants. Discussion of common conclusions led to the identification of four central underlying issues. The format of the workshop was changed in order to tackle these four key conclusions in depth through developing an 'Iceberg Exercise'. Starting from the 'tip' of the iceberg, the groups searched for the 'root causes' of some of the major weaknesses identified. Once the deeper issues were identified, group work then helped to identify recommendations that could address these weak areas.

During the final evaluation workshop, the draft national report was presented. Preliminary conclusions were 'tested' using a small group discussion technique, feedback and discussion in the plenary. The draft national report was then modified to incorporate feedback received during the workshop. An opportunity for the participants to share their general reflections on the significance of the evaluation exercise was also built into the workshop, with a view to determining implications for the future. The workshop report was written up, published and circulated widely to all diocesan committees and church structures, together with the final evaluation report.

Reflection and Analysis Phase

As mentioned above, the process of reflection and analysis started during the three-day final evaluation workshop. This was regarded as an introduction to the reflection and analysis on the findings of the evaluation and was designed to determine the action that had to be taken by way of follow-up. During the workshop the participants were assisted in identifying those conclusions and recommendations that pertained both to the national level and to their own dioceses, and in putting these in order of priority. Because of the magnitude of the information available from the evaluation, this has been the most difficult phase to implement.

One of the major issues that came out of the evaluation and was also re-emphasised in the final workshop was the need to formulate a 'vision statement' for the organisation from which concrete objectives and clear policy could be developed. In order to assist the dioceses to tackle this phase, the national office drew up the following outline of the discussion stages to be followed:

- discussion and drawing up of a vision statement;

- expressing or identifying the Commission's goals and objectives;

- reflecting on the present structures to determine how they respond to the objectives of the Commission;

- identifying programmes that would achieve the stated goals and objectives;

- developing policy for each of the identified programmes;

- considering the personnel required by the Commission for the effective implementation of the programmes.

It was intended that this framework for the reflection and analysis of the conclusions and recommendations would inevitably touch on a number of issues raised by the evaluation. This process has already started in the dioceses, in which special workshops are being organised to look at the results of the evaluation.

The dioceses find it easier to discuss those issues pertaining to their own situation than those at the national level. However, it is hoped that the above-mentioned guidelines will assist the dioceses not only to focus on diocesan issues but also on national issues. In the next executive meeting a deadline will be set for the finalisation of the discussions at diocesan level. Then a special meeting will be called to compile the outcome of the discussions and to draw up a plan on the implementation of the recommendations. It is anticipated that by the end of June the Commission will have finalised its deliberations.

A number of problems were identified through reflecting on the evaluation experience during the evaluation workshop and in subsequent discussions. The major problems encountered during the evaluation process included:

- the scale and complexity of the evaluation, as well as the large number of objectives to be addressed by a single evaluation;

- underestimating the time required to do the evaluation, especially given other work commitments of team members;

• cultural aspects were not sufficiently taken into consideration in the approach adopted.

• some technical problems arose in using structured interviews, such as inaccurate translation into vernacular languages, and insufficient training of team members;

• logistical difficulties, especially transport problems;

• different 'rhythms' of work and varied time commitments of the six different diocesan evaluation teams, leading to problems in timing and coordinating at national level;

• beneficiary groups not prepared for a participatory evaluation exercise.

Lessons From the Evaluation

It is quite clear from the previous evaluation and the present one that it is important to involve the personnel of the Commission at all levels in the formulation of the evaluation objectives (the project beneficiaries must also be involved as much as possible). Otherwise the is a danger that these personnel will regard the evaluation as just another exercise and ignore its findings, which is what happened with the first evaluation of the Commission.

Another lesson learnt is the importance of having clear evaluation objectives right from the beginning. This has been of great help in determining the type of information that should be solicited at various levels and also in determining the type of data gathering methods to be used. However, there is also the danger that in trying to establish clear objectives, one also ends up with a 'shopping list of objectives'. In responding to these objectives, a great deal of information is collected that will be difficult to interpret. It is very helpful for the organisation that is being evaluated to have clearly stated objectives and goals. This also applies to the individual programmes that are being evaluated. This gives the evaluators a point from which to start. Due to the lack of clarity in the Commission's objectives and those of its programmes, the resource person had to devote much time to go over the records of meetings and others documents in order to clarify the objectives.

The strength of a participatory approach to evaluation is that it motivates the various people involved to identify more strongly with it and see it through to its conclusion. However, it is a lengthy and more complex type of exercise than the more traditional approach to evaluation. There was a lot of openness in discussing the findings of the evaluation and nobody felt threatened by them. The question of involving partners in the different stages of the evaluation also meant that there were no differences in expectations between the Commission and its partners.

The process of evaluation has also benefitted the members of the organisation through consolidating the evaluation skills that had been gained in evaluation workshops organised by the Commission. It also created a certain degree of awareness among the staff of their own weaknesses and strong points. The need for treating evaluation as part and parcel of the Commission's programmes was also highlighted. Finally, it was also found that it was important to have a resource person who was sufficiently removed from the organisation to remain objective, but at the same time was sufficiently well informed about the Commission not to much time for familiarisation.

These are just some of the lessons learnt. The question of whether the evaluation has met its own aims cannot be fully answered until the whole exercise is complete. However, as far as meeting the objectives set for the evaluation is concerned, it is strongly felt that this has been accomplished.

What can we learn about the process of evaluation?

(i) Participatory evaluation, done in a holistic way, is a challenging, time-consuming and complex task. There is a strong tendency to underestimate the time and resource commitment involved. There are certain inherent tensions involved in any participatory evaluation that attempts to 'measure' effectiveness and efficiency:

• the 'process' orientation of participatory evaluation focuses on describing and interpreting qualitative phenomena;

• the 'outcome' orientation focuses on measuring results, usually assessed through the use of quantitative indicators.

Despite this tension, experience gained in the CADEC evaluation suggests that the dichotomy between 'qualitative' and 'quantitative' indicators is simplistic. Qualitative indicators can be quantified to assess effectiveness and quantitative indicators can be effectively used in participatory self-evaluation.

(ii) 'Insider' techniques associated with self-evaluation usually employ unstructured data gathering instruments, whereas 'outsider' techniques usually use structured ones. Although teams voiced difficulties in using some structured instruments, their experience suggests that, contrary to first impressions, unstructured data gathering instruments actually required more skill than structured ones. Perhaps for this reason, evaluation teams tended to emphasise the structured interviews, whereas information derived from unstructured techniques were somewhat down-played and inadequately reported.

(iii) The prevailing image of evaluation held by rural programme beneficiaries in Zimbabwe is that it is 'done' by outsiders. Past experience reinforces this image and can negatively affect the participatory nature of the process. Development agencies are seen as having resources and power and as a result evaluation and monitoring visits are seen as influencing access to 'rewards'. Despite careful attempts to guard against this, visits to project groups inevitably tend to raise expectations of further development assistance. This highlights the importance of participatory styles of evaluation being incorporated from the very beginning as part and parcel of the initiation of a social development project.

(iv) Cultural issues also exercise a profound influence on the participatory evaluation process and need to be anticipated in the planning phase. 'Politeness bias' coupled with the raised expectations of future assistance, leads to groups 'censuring' their information and opinions of effectiveness in a way believed to be most pleasing to the interviewers and most likely to improve the group's chances of securing further assistance. A range of cultural factors which limit participation by women as well as preference for indirect rather than direct style of questioning need to be clearly recognised and appropriate means taken to offset these difficulties.

(v) Although qualitative evaluation is said to be 'naturalistic' in that it avoids manipulating the programme or its participants for the purposes of evaluation (Oakley 1991), field experience indicated that it remains an unlikely ideal. The very presence of a 'visitor' (be it the fieldworker, or the evaluation team as a whole) inevitably creates a contrived situation, altering the project group dynamics and creating unintended expectations. Evaluation theory needs to be continually 'refined' in the face of practice.

(vi) The involvement of a fieldworker or other staff member with on-going knowledge of the project as a member of an evaluation team has a two-fold benefit when compared with a single outsider or insider;

• he/she is likely to be more sensitive to the differences between the 'contrived' situation and the day to day one;

• interaction with other members of a team can expand and challenge any 'subjective' interpretations he/she may make, helping the fieldworker to see the project in a new light.

(vii) The 'consciousness raising' and educative aspect of participatory evaluation is of great importance, both for the project managers and for the project beneficiaries. However, attention to this aspect requires a heavy investment of time during the field phase which must be allowed for in the work plan. Staff involvement heightens awareness of the weakness of existing programmes and sharpens critical skills. On-going reflection and sharing of team field experience is a vital component of the mutual learning exercise.

(viii) Good recording skills are essential in order to facilitate on-going project monitoring and evaluation and they cannot be totally compensated for by other means. However, in situations where the educational level and recording skills of team members vary considerably, division of tasks and good facilitation of the feedback process is vital to ensure that the experience, observations, and insights of all members are captured, whether or not they are able to record completely and accurately.

(ix) Although computer analysis is not usually associated with participatory types of evaluation, it can be a useful tool to store and retrieve information in ways that 'empower' rather than alienate evaluation teams. What is important is that the questions arise from the teams themselves and that the computerised information merely gives team members access to the data in a form that enables them to answer their own questions.

(x) At what stage is it best to train evaluation teams in data analysis? Experience gained in the CADEC evaluation suggests that data analysis skills are effectively learnt by 'hands on' type of work with the actual data they themselves have gathered during the evaluation. This heightens the motivation of the team, as they learn skills that help them to interpret their own findings and draw their own conclusions. However, lack of training in data analysis skills prior to data collection makes it more difficult for team members to realise the importance of accurate and complete recording of information while in the field.

Group Discussion on Case Study

Veronica Bland and Cosmas Wakatama made a substantial presentation of the Zimbabwe case study. The study had been circulated beforehand and group members had the opportunity to read it. The whole exercise had been one not only of the evaluation of CADEC's work but also one of institution building; and interestingly this institution building concerned not only CADEC but also the network of structures at the community level with whom CADEC worked. In their overall presentation, Veronica and Cosmas emphasised the different actors (local people, groups and agency staff) who had participated in the evaluation exercise and the emphasis in the evaluation methodology upon interviews since there had been a distinct lack of information which had been collected over time upon which to base the evaluation. They stressed also the deliberate attempts in the evaluation exercise to achieve a balance between the quantitative and the qualitative outcomes of CADEC's work. The notion of qualitative change had presented more difficulties, but it was felt that CADEC had been quite innovative in the ways it had sought to assess, such as in the use of pictures. In general terms the evaluation had gone quite smoothly and there had been no major hitches or blocks in its implementation.

During a more general discussion on the paper presenting the CADEC evaluation, the following kinds of issues or points were made:

(i) In financial, time and labour terms, the CADEC evaluation had been quite costly. The exercise had taken several months, it had involved a whole range of people from outside consultants to local level community enumerators, and it had not been cheap. All of this raised the question of whether, in terms of the end product, CADEC could have achieved the same results with a less ambitious evaluation design? The answer is probably 'yes'. In term of the future development of CADEC's work, the elaborate administrative and logistical support was considered worth-while since it produced a highly participative evaluation exercise. It was felt that the gains from this participation did out weigh the quite considerable costs.

(ii) In terms of the evaluation methodology, the evaluation exercise had underlined the central role of workshops in terms of bringing participants together, involving them in the exercise, and structuring a number of concrete evaluation orientated activities such as group analysis and reflection upon particular aspects of CADEC's work. Interestingly, however, it had also been found that 'unstructured' research methods had been the more difficult to apply in the evaluation exercise. Both enumerators and respondents were much more at ease and able to handle and respond to structured interview schedules, but they had found it relatively more difficult when asked 'open-ended' questions or when asked to reflect or comment upon a particular aspect of CADEC's work.

(iii) A substantial discussion took place on the 'Field Methods' section of the CADEC evaluation paper. This dealt with the issue of indicators and criteria employed by the evaluation to 'measure' the indicators. In the whole area, it was felt that the CADEC evaluation had broken new ground in that it appeared quite successfully to have identified relevant 'phenomena' by which the evaluation indicators, and in particular the qualitative ones, could be 'measured'. This issue of relevant 'phenomena' was at the heart of qualitative evaluation since, without some observable means of 'measuring' a qualitative indicator, it would be impossible in any scientific way to assess the outcome of a particular aspect of the qualitative change which had occurred.

The evaluators confirmed that the evaluation had been able to come to grips quite concretely with the notion of qualitative indicators but suggested that, on reflection, it might have been better to have done a preliminary run with the indicators before the main evaluation. They had not done this but now realise that it might have been useful in terms of helping to define some of the more qualitative indicators used. For example, such terms as 'self-reliance', 'livelihood' and 'self-esteem' are notoriously difficult to define in a way that, universally, is culturally acceptable. A main stumbling block was that participants had very differing understandings of such terms. This was a major conclusion of the evaluation and any qualitative evaluation exercise should examine the issue in detail before launching on information collection.

(iv) On balance it was felt that the employment by CADEC of a main 'resource person' to facilitate and direct the whole evaluation exercise was appropriate. Without such a person, it probably would have been impossible to bring the whole exercise to a timely and meaningful outcome. Such a person needed to combine not only knowledge of the overall processes of evaluation, in both quantitative and qualitative dimensions, but also the skills to direct qualified enumerators, and to elicit community involvement. It is probably unwise to think in term of drawing up a list of the more useful personal attributes. In many ways there is an element of 'luck' in finding the right resource person for a particular evaluation.

(v) A major issue emerging from the CADEC evaluation concerned the interpretation and use of qualitative data. In this it had to be concluded that the CADEC evaluation had not been entirely successful. However, the problem of the interpretation of qualitative data was a widely recognised one. Some research had been undertaken on the matter but, in general, there were still few proven experiences in the evaluation of development programmes. The issue had been noted by the CADEC evaluation and it was hoped that future research might begin to help unravel this complex issue.

In conclusion the question was asked whether the CADEC exercise had produced a 'model for evaluation'. There can be no emphatic answer to this question since it is debatable whether there could ever be 'models' for such a complex activity as evaluation. However, it was felt that CADEC had pushed several issues forward. In particular it had successfully held together a complex exercise, involving both quantitative and qualitative aspects, involving both professionals and rural communities, and there had been a positive and concrete outcome. One particular outcome would be the production of a basic evaluation manual. More broadly the evaluation had made a substantial contribution to our understanding of the problems associated with qualitative evaluation.

3.2 THE PROCESS OF EVALUATING SOCIAL
DEVELOPMENT: PRAJWALA, INDIA

R. Monhanraj
Prajwala, India

Introduction

Prajwala is an initiative to encourage peoples' movements among the marginalised sections of Indian society. The involvement of Prajwala has thus been a continuously emerging process, with its own dynamics. Prajwala has attached great importance to evaluating this emerging process. This case study is an effort to describe how this evaluation has been undertaken.

Prajwala was initiated in 1985 by a group of individuals with a common concern for strengthening the marginalised sections of Indian society. It is registered with the Registrar of societies and with the Home Ministry of the Government of India. This group now consists of eleven persons and forms the board of Prajwala. The board itself has been an emerging body and the executive committee is democratically elected from among the members. The committee meets twice a year to review and guide the direction and involvement of Prajwala.

The present team consists of twelve full time organisers and ten part time volunteers, along with two administrative personnel. Care has always been taken to ensure that the team of Prajwala is also part of the target population. This ensures that a cadre is developed, leadership built up and an investment is made in human personnel. This is means of ensuring long term continuity in the process. For two years Prajwala depended upon friends and well wishers to help support its work. Resources were also mobilised for specific programmes from the various departments of state and the Government of India. However, since 1987 the day to day work of Prajwala has been largely made possible by the support of Christian Aid.

Prajwala works in two mandals of Chittoor District, Andhra Pradesh, South India (a mandal is an administrative unit of the Government). These mandals are S.R. Puram Mandal, which covers 168 sq.kms. and has a population of 28,100, and Karvetinagar Mandal which covers 323 sq.kms. and has a population of 38,287. The target population of Prajwala's work are the marginalised sections of this society. Our understanding of the marginalised has not, however, been static, and we have found that there are different layers among the marginalised. In 1985, when we initiated the work, we understood the 'poor' as a single block of the 'marginalised' based mostly on the economic factor. However, by 1987, we realised that the 'Dalits' form another deeper layer among the poor. The world 'dalit' means broken. These are the communities who have been historically exploited and kept outside the caste system as the 'untouchables'. They remain so even to this day. Since 1987 our focus has been more on this group.

The Dalits in the two mandals that Prajwala works have the following characteristics.

- they belong to the Mala and Madiga communities;

- they constitute 29% of the total population;

- 95% of them are agricultural labourers who either do not own land or only have small tracts of land below 2 hectares;

- their literacy level and representation in the different walks of life is much lower than the national average.

Vision and Direction

The vision of Prajwala is to have an Indian society in which the marginalised sections will be able to play a participatory role in the construction of a just society. We do not see this as a movement only by the marginalised sections also requiring all other sections of society to participate. The direction of Prajwala has been to initiate, encourage and support a mass movement, especially of the Dalit population.

The objectives of Prajwala's work are:

(i) To develop leadership among the agricultural labourers, which is both democratic and sensitive to people and their problems.

(ii) To help the Dalits in analysing the existing Indian socio-political system and the forces that oppress them.

(iii) To assist people in development programmes through mobilisation of Government programmes.

(iv) To organise people to come together and collectively solve their problems by developing a forum of their own.

(v) To help Dalits to participate more fully in the social, political, economic life of Indian society.

Strategy

Prajwala's strategy is to organise the Dalit population into a strong body so as to enable them to participate meaningfully in the social, economic and political aspects of Indian life. The caste system has become a web of social oppression for the Dalits, controlling every aspect of life and reducing the Dalits to the status of untouchables in Indian society. This has deep personal, moral and psychological consequences for them. In response, Prajwala has concentrated its efforts in the following areas: building up local leadership; education; creating awareness; analysing the contextual situation of the Dalits; and in assisting them to organise themselves together. Various measures have also been taken to affirm the Dalit culture, and community and individual consciousness.

Another significant aspect which affects the lives of the Dalits is the increasing number of atrocities against them. In the past, this violence had been latent and usually expressed in terms of stringent social and economic sanctions. Prajwala, along with neighbouring groups and through networks established for this purpose, have worked to strengthen the people to confront those forces and agents responsible for the atrocities.

On the economic front the strategy is to use constitutionally available methods to help Dalits. The focus of this strategy has been to obtain land, to protect land, to increase wages, to mobilise resources from the Government, to introduce new skills, to encourage community enterprises and collective efforts, and to support educational programmes so that they will be able to improve their economic status.

In the political area, Dalits have not, as yet, participated in any decision making role in the general community. However, they are organised to participate in the elected bodies like the Panchayat and local societies, and they are also organised to put up their own candidates and participate responsibly. This has initiated a process whereby the Dalits do have a voice in the running of their society. Campaigns and mass mobilisations have also been undertaken in order to influence public opinion.

Prajwala realises the need for wider intervention, at least at the district and state level. Hence Prajwala is involved in networking with other groups within the district and state. A common platform for agricultural labourers has been initiated at the state level by a number of voluntary organisations, who have formed the *Andhra Pradesh Rashtra Vyavasaya Coolieala Samakhya* (A.P. State Agricultural Labourers Federation). This has the explicit purpose of initiating a trade union of the agricultural labourers. Through networking efforts a number of crucial issues have been addressed, such as 'untouchability', the minimum wage, employment guarantees and land issues. Efforts are also made to develop a district perspective for planning development along with partner and donor groups.

Concept of Evaluation

Prajwala has been involved with agricultural labourers in strengthening their organisations. This has been a dynamic process, which has lead us to intervene in the lives of the marginalised sections through various means and through various organisations. Evaluation in Prajwala has been an exercise in this continuously emerging process of involvement.

Right from the inception of Prajwala, we have been involved in a continuous process of reflection to discern if our programmes and activities lead us to our objectives, and if our involvement could help us realise the aims we have set. Simultaneously we have also been in a continuous process of checking whether the issues that we are involved in, and the objectives and aims that we have set, are relevant to the marginalised sections. The whole question of 'who are the marginalised?' has also been to a great extent continuously sharpened.

Tools of Evaluation

In undertaking evaluation we have also realised the importance of developing and using appropriate tools to gauge and value the emerging process. While social development indicators are difficult to delineate, an evaluation process which is not sensitive and which cannot visualise the possible mode of evolution will easily miss the point.

Essentially Prajwala has been involved in two types of evaluation:

(i)   On-going Evaluation Process: *OEP*

(ii) Time-bound Evaluation Exercise: *TEE*

Of the two, OEP has contributed more in guiding the direction of Prajwala. It is a group exercise in which Prajwala is involved and takes place in various forms. The TEE, on the other hand, is mostly an external intervention, decided on by Prajwala and the donor organisation. It has contributed to validating the decisions that have been arrived at through OEP. TEE has also gone beyond the immediate issues and on-going programmes and has helped in clarifying the wider vision and possible modes of evolution. It has also strengthened the resource base through the provision of data and the involvement of resource persons.

On-Going Evaluation Process

From its experiences of the past years, Prajwala stresses the important role played by OEP. OEP is an internal process where the Prajwala team comes together to reflect upon, guide and plan its involvement. Major shifts in programmes and direction in Prajwala are decided upon after OEP exercises.

Two examples are given to illustrate the value of the OEP. Prajwala began its involvement in eight villages, trying to totally identify with the people and to effectively bring about change. After a year of involvement, it became clear from the OEP that it was not possible to tackle the core issues affecting people through focusing on just eight villages. The necessity of involvement in a wider geo-politically viable area was realised. Thus it was only through the OEP that we consciously started involving ourselves in a wider level of the mandal.

As another example we can outline the sharpening of Prajwala's focus on Dalit issues through the OEP. In the earlier period, poverty was defined more in a class context, but through OEP we began to realise the relevance of a caste/class analysis in our society. This lead to a commitment to develop Dalit consciousness in our work. The OEP has proved a crucial, continuous evaluation process which helped ensure the relevance of our involvement.

Time-bound Evaluation Exercise

While OEP is the important method by which we could contextualise our involvement, this is ideally supplemented by TEE. The role of TEE is to check OEP, and to validate it. With the help and expertise of external resource persons, it has been possible to impartially and objectively view the process and make any necessary changes in direction. TEE has assisted Prajwala in looking at its strengths and weaknesses, its outside influences and its external resources, and to deepen, as well as broaden, its horizon. It becomes clear that both OEP and TEE are two sides of the same coin. There is the need to periodically countercheck OEP, while TEE is meaningless unless supported by a regular OEP.

In the experience of Prajwala there have been several time-bound evaluation exercises carried out with the help of external resource persons. However, this does not need to be done only by external resource persons. TEE can also be done internally, but this differs from OEP in that it takes a particular point in time as the cut-off and reflects back at the whole process that preceded it. Since Prajwala is a social developmental initiative, TEE needed to look at the pivotal aspects of organisation that had taken place up to that point in time. Here we realised the importance of the type of tools that are needed to gauge these pivotal aspects of the process.

Preparatory Phase

Planning for evaluation is necessary for both OEP and TEE and is a very crucial aspect to the whole process. Planning involves; time scheduling, identifying the participants, developing the terms of reference and issues to be identified, the collection of information and data, deciding on the relevant tools, methods of reporting and the follow up.

OEP is carried out both periodically and in relation to specific issues or programmes. The following questions were asked during the monthly reviews of the team, the six monthly meetings with the board the evaluation of our involvement is an integral part of discussions:

* to what extent where we able to carry out the activities?

* to what extent were these activities helpful in realising the objectives?

* to what extent did the objectives coincide with the people's aspirations, issues and needs?

Similarly OEP is also carried out after each programme, or after each issue is identified and agreed. For instance, in 1986 in the initial stages of our involvement, a programme was set up to provide community irrigation well. When we were nearing completion of the programme the team members of Prajwala, as well as two other neighbouring organisations who were involved in this programme, had a combined OEP exercise. We discussed the relevance of this programme to local people:

* whom did this programme benefit?

* in what way did the programme benefit them—as passive recipients or by empowering them?

* did it strengthen the entire community in their struggle—or did it create individual assets?

* what image of the organisation was projected—as a benefactor, or partners in struggle?

Once this OEP had been undertaken, the relevant data was collected. Here it must be noted that we were not focusing exclusively on land development programmes in isolation to the other essential processes that are set in the objectives. Therefore the data that was collected related to:

- the resources available within the community, such as what percentage of people had control over them;

- the main issues faced by the people such as the extent of caste discrimination and marginalisation;

- the power politics that emerged in relation to this programme;

- the extent to which the programme encouraged community participation;

- the role played by Prajwala team.

In this process the community leaders, the participants in the programme, the organisers and team leaders involved, from both Prajwala and two neighbouring groups, sat together to evaluate the process in response to the data collected.

Similarly there have been two TEE interventions within Prajwala since 1985. The need for a second TEE was identified by Prajwala in mid 1989. This was based on the realisation that it would be helpful to validate the OEP. The decision was communicated to Christian Aid, who agreed with the importance of conducting a TEE for assessing how, and how far, the objectives of Prajwala have been achieved. It also stressed the importance of TEE in order to decide the future partnership between Prajwala and Christian Aid.

Consequently, a TEE was planned for December, 1989, with the following objectives:

- to validate the On-going Evaluation Process (OEP) in Prajwala;

- to reconfirm the focus of Prajwala's objectives, and recommend any necessary changes;

- to assess Prajwala's abilities and strategies to take action in the direction recommended by the TEE carried out in 1987;

- to reconfirm the developmental consensus between Christian Aid and Prajwala.

Based on this consensus, the facilitators for the TEE were chosen with care. Christian Aid, understanding the context of the TEE suggested one of the facilitators. The facilitators chosen were associates of Prajwala who were familiar not only with its vision, objectives and activities, but even with individual members of the core team. The second important criteria was the facilitators' knowledge and understanding about the geo-political context of the area. One of the facilitators had an on-going involvement with about five to six other programmes in the Chittoor district.

In order to reach an effective outcome of TEE, it was necessary to establish consensus on the objectives of the exercise between the board members, the core team and Christian Aid. Objectives for the exercise were worked out initially by the core team. It was then communicated to the board members and Christian Aid, and suggestions from both sources were incorporated. As its main point of reference the TEE took into consideration the objectives of Prajwala, as stated in its proposal for Christian Aid. Prajwala had developed a fairly clear direction for its work and hence the objectives were clearly stated. This helped the process of qualitative assessment.

The TEE drew upon available secondary data, as well as primary data generated through the TEE exercise. The facilitators spent time going through all available information such as the initial survey records, the minutes of core team meetings, the minutes of the village level meetings, records of board meetings, and the proposal to, and correspondence with, Christian Aid. The facilitators themselves also counter-checked and updated their understanding of the geo-political trends in the Chittoor district. Finally it was decided that the TEE would not include accounts or financial aspects, since there were being done separately under the financial accompaniment system of Christian Aid.

Execution Phase

The execution phase in both OEP and TEE included sessions of discussions and reflections. One important factor here was the selection of indicators to assess the impact of involvement as well as the criteria through which we could assess the importance of this involvement. In the execution phase of the evaluation Prajwala began by focusing on local popular organisations, know as sanghams. However, many of us in Prajwala as well as the neighbouring groups felt that the 'sangham' approach was limited and would not give us a information on a wider geo-political area. In response to this, an OEP was undertaken to search for viable alternative models to strengthen the peoples' organisational process.

The execution of the 'sangham' approach included planning, collecting initial data on how sanghams were effective, what issues sangham could or could not take up and what issues were identified by the local population. With this data in hand meetings were held at different levels. Initially a meeting of group leaders and resource persons was held to examine the alternate models for involvement. The advantages and disadvantages of the alternate model of organising people through trade unions was discussed.

Equipped with this information, further discussions were held with the team members, neighbouring groups and community leaders of the local population. Further doubts were expressed, but at the same time a renewed commitment was made to explore all possibilities that could take Prajwala nearer to its aims. Here comparisons were made with various existing unions and the relevance of a union to agricultural labourers. These discussions were precipitated and recorded in the form of a report and were presented to the board of Prajwala.

Finally at the board meeting in November 1990 it was decided to release part of the team to actively initiate and promote a trade union of agricultural labourers. It was decided that Prajwala would play a supporting role to the peoples' organisations, while the trade union would be a mass organisation having constitutional validity to effect some of the changes. In effect the OEP methodology of execution is clearly expressed in this process. The team, the board and the neighbouring groups came together to decide on changes in their course and roles.

The TEE execution in 1989 was facilitated by the two resource persons, but with the full participation of the Prajwala team. The terms of reference (TOR) were agreed out of a participatory exercise with the core group. Based on a 'perception–reflection' methodology, the developmental frame of Prajwala was converted into pictures by means of which the members of the group were helped to identify the various areas related to the TOR. The outcome was offered for reflection to the board members and Christian Aid, and suggestions were incorporated and before finalising the final form of the TOR. The facilitators conceptualised the TOR into their two inter-related components; ideology, and action. The entire facilitation process was based on these two inter-related components. The role of facilitation on each of the two components was divided between the two facilitators.

Although the TEE had a planned schedule of five days, the methodology and reflection content for each inter-action was flexible and open. The outcome of one discussion was used to decide the methodology and content for the following one. This process can be explained as follows:

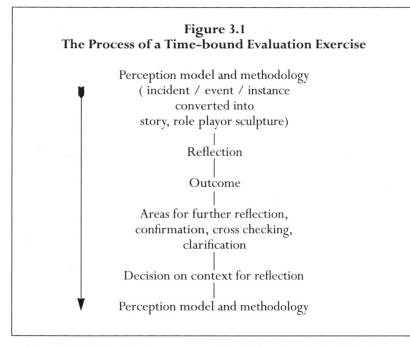

Figure 3.1
The Process of a Time-bound Evaluation Exercise

Perception model and methodology
(incident / event / instance
converted into
story, role play or sculpture)
|
Reflection
|
Outcome
|
Areas for further reflection,
confirmation, cross checking,
clarification
|
Decision on context for reflection
|
Perception model and methodology

The schedule for the five days was decided and maintained by the core group. They decided on when and where to meet and what should be discussed. The role of the facilitators in this process was to offer different perspectives on Prajwala's objectives and programmes. As necessary, theoretical inputs were provided to reinforce and to activate the reflection process.

The five days schedule was largely based upon an examination of the activities which form the regularly scheduled activities of Prajwala. Consequently, all the actors involved, such as the core group, staff group and community representatives, had their contribution and role in the TEE process. The members of the Prajwala board were also involved at the final stage of reflection and in making recommendations.

Two sets of indicators were developed for the TEE:

(i) Indicators for awareness and the internalisation of the education process.

(ii) Indicators for the materialistic aspects of development.

For the first set of indicators five stages were formulated. These were based upon a group consensus that awareness and education are measurable not just at the giving end but also at the receiving end.

Stage I: *Information Level*

The message given remains as information.
'Yes, there is some form of caste discrimination here. We are affected'.

Stage II: *Experiential Level*

The message goes to the level of recollection of experiences.
'About 5 years ago in our village there was an atrocity committed by the Reddys on the Dalits. Two of my family members were also attacked'.

Stage III: *Awareness Level*

At this stage, the situation is not seen as an isolated incident but as part of a system.
'These atrocities do not affect everybody. They affect us because we are poor. It is the Dalits who are affected. The rich are not affected'.

Stage IV: *Personal Motivation Level*

This is the level in which the individual is personally motivated to play a role.
'Atrocities are a recurring phenomenon. They happen every time anybody dares to question! Each time the repercussions are more severe. At this rate, not only me but my children and future generation will be affected. Some thing must be done. I would like to participate in actions that confront these atrocities'.

Stage V: *Cooperation and Leadership*

There are two levels of motivation for participating:

(a) 'I would like to play a lead role to prevent atrocities'
(Leadership potential)

(b) 'I would like to be a member of a group working to prevent atrocities'

(Motivation to Co-operate)

For indicators related to the fulfilment of material needs, the developmental frame of Prajwala was used. The following indicators were developed:

(i) The extent to which the people's immediate needs have been fulfilled through:

- government resources

- external resources

- peoples' contributions

(ii) The ways and the extent to which the meeting of material needs contribute towards the organisational process of the people.

- if so how and how much?

- if not, why?

(iii) The implication for local people of material needs being fulfilled:

- the condition of satisfaction/fulfilment/complacency.

- the tendency for dependency creation.

- self confidence and motivation for more collective action towards meeting of more needs.

In addition to these indicators, some basic principles were adopted in the methodology of the evaluation, including:

No Pressure of Time: It was ensured that the group were not subjected to any pressure of time. The evaluation sessions were at the time and pace of the group. Longer group sessions were inter-spaced with cultural action, such as group songs, games and folk stories.

No Necessary Conclusion: The evaluation exercise based on the principle that any discussion or reflection need not necessarily be subjected to conclusion. When there were contradictions, the divergence was acknowledged. It was also hoped that the opinions expressed did not become personal against one another, but this situation could not be completely avoided.

Verbal Expression Versus Visual Expressions: In rural communities, verbal expressions relate to cultural influences, such as those based on age, social identity in the village, and the ability to sing and speak publicly. In order to ensure that every member of the group understood the context, the group members were encouraged to express their understanding and opinions using visual forms, such as pictures, song, role-play and sculptures.

Reporting Phase

Reporting in OEP is mostly done in the form of minutes of meetings. These also include up to date information on particular issues or programmes. These latter are also reported on in the form of reports by the team members for further reference, reflection and follow up. All of this reports are also presented to the board for reflection and follow up. When the OEP is between village leaders or in very small groups, even verbal reports are used and accepted as sufficient.

The reporting for TEE is more formalised. An elaborate report was prepared for the 1989 TEE. Since the objective of the TEE was two fold—firstly as a requirement for Prajwala and secondly as an administrative requirement of Christian Aid—the report of the TEE was done in two forms:

Exercise Report: For the use in Prajwala, all the exercise papers, charts, and sheets were preserved as the report of the TEE. A summary form of this report was selected to be used for further OEP. This is in the local language of Telugu and was used by the group as a basis for continued monitoring, reflection and changing direction. The group also used this report as a base material to make the action plans for the next three years of work (1990–1993).

Administrative Report: For administrative and documentation purposes, an elaborate report in English was prepared by the facilitators, the contents of which were agreed beforehand. This report contained an elaborate analysis of the various ideological and theoretical perspectives reflected on during the exercise. The administrative report was presented to the board members of Prajwala for analysis and scrutiny. The board invited the facilitators to a meeting in which various contents of the report were clarified. Based on the above clarifications, the recommendations were then analysed, and a copy of the report was also made available to

Christian Aid, who along with the Prajwala used this report as a basic document for the programme partnership for the next three years of 1990-1993.

The board realised that it would be helpful if the facilitators of the evaluation could accompany Prajwala over the following few years in order that the two inter-related components of ideology and operational forms could be systematised and strengthened. A request was made to Christian Aid about the need for this accompaniment, and they agreed. The two facilitators also agreed to accompany the project.

This agreement has been continued up to the time of writing this case study. The two facilitators have visited Prajwala once every three months for a duration of three to four days. The time has been spent informally: sharing opinions, visiting villages, talking with community representatives, debating on certain aspects of ideological and operational forms; and training the members of the group in analytical as well as operational skills.

Reflection and Analysis Phase

The major changes of direction and focus taken by Prajwala have all been achieved by reflection and analysis of the evaluation process which has included both OEP and TEE. The former has been a continuous process of reflection and analysis. It can be looked at as a spiral where we move from one point to another in a continuously emerging process. OEP has been the major tool which has helped us in the development of our work. As an example we can look at the community irrigation wells programme. The analysis and reflections on this programme through the OEP came to the following conclusions:

• land is not available to the majority of the poor Dalits;

• those who could make use of the programme were inevitably the better off;

• the ones who utilised the programme did gain considerably from it, both through the mobilisation of their involvement in the programme as well as in economic terms. However to the general community this was not an empowering process;

• the image of Prajwala was considerably boosted as an organisation that had some power and could get things done.

Based on these reflections and analysis at the various levels, a consensus was reached that Prajwala should focus more on the struggle and empowering aspect for the present, and on mobilising people to utilise resources. It should not be seen as the direct provider of material assistance.

The second example concerns the unionisation of agricultural labourers. The results of the reflection-analysis process through OEP were as follows:

• on analysis, it was clear that the 'sangham' model of organising had a number of limitations that could to some extent be overcome through unionisation;

• it was also noted that the unionisation process with agricultural labourers was quite distinct from that of workers in the industrial sector;

• on the question of who will lead the union, there was a general consensus that some people from the programme were needed in the initial phase. Hence the decision to release a few colleagues from Prajwala.

Thus it can be confidently claimed that reflection and analysis through OEP has been quite crucial in deepening the involvement of Prajwala. It was through OEP for example, that shifts were made from the focus on eight to ten villages to a wider geopolitical area, from a class perspective to caste and class perspective, and towards a more sharpened focus on the Dalits and on unions.

OEP has involved various sections of people–local people, the team, group leaders, and neighbouring organisations. The exercises provided the opportunity for the expression of individual perceptions and understandings which together helped in clarifying common perceptions, creating awareness and developing a genuine bond between the different actors. It has ensured that our work was relevant to the times and to the people. This was validated by the TEE and still continues to be the key factor in the involvement of Prajwala.

Reflection and analysis in the TEE was also carried out at different levels, although it was more restricted by time. The relevance and efficacy of TEE was amply evident from the reflections and analysis. It provided the scope for validating the OEP and the involvement of Prajwala. The TEE enabled a wider understanding of the interrelations to be developed between the localised situation and its linkages to the wider society. The TEE in general has achieved its aim in both external and internal environments. Externally it enabled Prajwala to update its analysis and understanding of the community situations at the macro level. Internally the exercise helped the team at Prajwala to have stronger belief in its vision and reassure themselves of where the organisation was going. TEE also helped Prajwala in terms of understanding the operational implications of a larger organisations such as the labour union. This also lead to the Prajwala team leader to opt out of the Prajwala structure in order to take full time responsibility as the secretary in the union. Finally TEE has also been helpful in that the evaluation report was used for further reflections in the OEP. Continuity has also been assured through the system of accompaniment by the facilitators.

Final Comments

A major conclusion of the whole exercise was the need to develop relevant evaluation tools in keeping with cultural factors. In a short time, communication can be effectively guided by the use of tools in keeping with both the evolutionary process of the programme and the local culture. It was also concluded that the 'Perception–Reflection' methodology model used in the TEE had been very helpful. Another learning point was the need to understand the local situation within the macro context. The team and the leaders need to continuously upgrade their understanding of this aspect and guide the programme accordingly.

The major problem encountered in the TEE was the time constraint. TEE tries to halt a process and reflect on it backwards over a period of time. Though it is possible to achieve the objectives set in terms of a process, the constraint of time was evident. To some extent the accompaniment programme will seek to overcome this problem. It was also felt that in the area where the localised situations were interlinked with larger, national situations, the evaluation tools used were inadequate. People had difficulty in internalising the concepts about larger, national situations. Hence it was felt that more visuals and charts were needed to help people participate especially in the field of social development programmes. As local people have been involved in a continuously emerging process, it was felt that there would be a continuing need to develop appropriate evaluation tools to monitor this process.

3.3 THE INTERNATIONAL CENTRE FOR EDUCATION AND HUMAN DEVELOPMENT, CINDE, COLOMBIA AND THE EVALUTION OF THE PROGRAMME TO IMPROVE EDUCATION, HEALTH AND THE ENVIRONMENT (PROMESA)

Glen Nimnicht, Lydia Hearn and Alejandro Acosta
International Centre for Education and Human Development (CINDE)
Colombia

Introduction

Over the past twelve years the International Centre for Education and Human Development, CINDE, based primarily in Colombia has been developing and implementing a variety of home-based, community-based, and complementary approaches to early childhood care and education. The main strategy has been to enable parents and the communities to attend better to the needs of their children. These programmes have been implemented in different regions of the country over different periods of time, and have been extensively evaluated. This is a summary of the evaluation of PROMESA, CINDE's largest and most long-term programme, situated in the Chocó on the Pacific Coast of Colombia, in a hot, humid and isolated area, which is accessible only by boat or small plane.

Project PROMESA was designed initially to evaluate an alternative approach to meeting the needs of the healthy development of young children. Embedded in PROMESA was a concept of community development based upon the notion that individuals must be involved in their own process of development, and that for this development to occur there must be a simultaneous process of change in the intellectual, physical, economic and socio-cultural aspects of life. Moreover, the project stressed the importance of developing in individuals the ability to solve problems and think logically, and to build up the self-confidence required to carry out such changes.

Thus, from the perspective of Project PROMESA neither the top down nor the bottom up approaches to social development were totally satisfactory. Social development had to be done in cooperation with the community, but at the same time there was some need for outside input. Instead two basic objectives became central to the programme:

(i) An immediate effort to improve the local environment for the healthy development of young children, by enabling the parents and members of the community to become the key educators in this process.

(ii) A more long-term objective to enable the parents and community to become organised so that they can continue and build upon this process of improving the environment for their children.

During its first ten years, PROMESA was sponsored primarily by two Dutch organisations, the Bernard van Leer Foundation and CEBEMO. The project started in 1978 with 100 families in four small farming and fishing villages. It now serves a total of approximately 4,000 families both along the coast and in the interior regions of Chocó, while variations of its approach, or components of it, are being implemented in other parts of the country and even in other countries.

The programme began by encouraging groups of mothers from the poorest sectors of the communities to stimulate the physical and intellectual development of their pre-school children by playing games with them in the home. Gradually, during the meetings, the mothers started to identify other problems related to topics such as health, nutrition, environmental sanitation, vocational training, income generation, and cultural activities. Over time, therefore, as individuals gained confidence and developed a greater understanding of their overall needs, PROMESA expanded into an integrated community development project, with the entire community participating in one or more aspects of the programme, and with some of the initial mothers becoming *promotoras*, or community leaders. The various activities which evolved as the programme developed can be classified into four basic components: socio-intellectual, physical, productive, and socio-cultural.

The component of socio-intellectual development has involved the continuous education of adults through workshops, self-study groups and follow-up activities aimed at improving the quality of family interactions and life. Most of the participants are parents of children from under ten years old, who are interested in improving the quality of the physical and psychological environment where they live, and in enhancing the development of their children. The education for these parents involves programmes to learn how to provide a healthy environment for young children, vocational training, and education for leaders. It has also involved the development of a set of educational toys and games to improve the interaction between the parents and their children and to encourage processes of logical thinking. Pre-school and nutrition centres have also been organised and run by the community, with the support of local institutional agents.

The physical development component includes health, nutrition, and environmental sanitation. A primary health care system, administered by the community has been one of important outcomes of this component.

The productive component has supported the organisation of groups interested in improving their income generating, organisational and administrative capacities. It has included the establishment of revolving funds and activities aimed at improving the quality of work and the marketing of their products.

The socio-cultural component has aimed to foster the organisation of activities designed to strengthen the cultural identity of the groups, especially by recovering and reviewing important aspects of their past history and culture. Part of this component includes the formation of groups whose objective is to organise and become involved in different cultural activities, such as drama and music, traditional games, and the study of traditional myths, legends, and medical practices.

Four particular management features have had an important impact on the success of the programme, and deserve to be highlighted:

(i) The *promotoras*, many of them mothers from the poorest sectors of the communities, have been the main educational agents in the programme;

(ii) The external agent, CINDE, has not been directly involved with the community, but rather their role has been to educate the *promotoras* and other community leaders and local politicians, to serve as facilitators in the development process, and to act as a link with other institutions;

(iii) Emphasis from the outset on inter-institutional coordination at the local and regional level has contributed a great deal to the success of the programme;

(iv) Despite the impoverished area in which the programme is located, attention has primarily been directed towards educational and organisational processes.

Another crucial element in the programme is that from its beginning, parents have been involved in different aspects of programme planning and implementation. This has varied from community to community according to the socio-cultural and political variables affecting the project at different moments. In fact, the parents themselves (or other community leaders) have been the main educational agents and organisers of the programme. Furthermore, most of project activities have started outside the school or other formal systems.

The Local Context

Project PROMESA is located in the state of Chocó, on the Pacific coast of Colombia, just south of Panamá. It is a tropical rainforest zone with one of the highest levels of rainfall in the world and is an inaccessible and largely uninhabited region. The few communities in the region are made up of largely of black descendants of African slaves who form 80% of the population, with the Embera Indians forming 7% of the population.

Economically, Chocó is one of the poorest states in Colombia. Its industrial sector is limited to a liquor manufacturing plant and a few cottage industries typical of the informal sector. Agriculture features rudimentary crops such as corn, yucca, rice and some fruits, while hunting, fishing, and logging are also done on a elementary basis. However, beef, dairy herds, and draught animals are virtually non-existent. Subsistence farming and fishing continue to be the major form of livelihood, and 56% of families have a monthly income below the national minimum wage for rural areas (us$40).

The region is extremely isolated; there are only two roads into the state and these are both inadequate and go only as far as Quibdó, the state capital, situated in the interior. However, there is no road or river link to the communities on the Pacific coast. At present this part of Chocó can only be reached by air or sea, making transportation routes slow and expensive. This problem of transportation is aggravated by the poor communication services. There are still few telephone lines and mail is slow.

The harsh environment, and the poor water and sanitary conditions, makes diseases like malaria, gastro-enteritis and parasites endemic in the region. When the project began in 1979, the infant mortality rate for the region was over 150 per 1,000 live births, a rate three time higher than the national average, which today is 57 per 1,000 live births. Moreover, at this time there were few hospitals or health posts, and those that did exist rarely had doctors, equipment or medicines. Sanitary conditions in the region were also poor; less than 5% of the houses in any of the communities where Project PROMESA began had latrines or running water, adding to the lack of hygiene and spread of disease.

Illiteracy also plagued 57% of the population in the region, a rate four times higher than the national average. In 1980, pre-school programmes reached only 0.15% of the children of pre-school age. Only 60% of school aged children enrolled in primary education and of those, only 4% in rural areas and 32% in urban areas completed fifth grade.

The Concept of Evaluation used in Project PROMESA

From the beginning, evaluation has been an integral part of Project PROMESA. It has been seen not only as an instrument to improve and assess the project as an alternative model for meeting the needs of the healthy development of young children, but also, as a fundamental strategy to build autonomy, self-direction and self-reliance at the individual and community level.

For this reason, the evaluation process used by CINDE has had various components and objectives. On the one hand, evaluation has been used as an 'on-going strategy' to encourage individuals to reflect on their situation and to become aware not only of their needs but also of their ability to take action to overcome their short-comings. Along the same lines, the process of self-evaluation and monitoring of the programme has served to raise and maintain motivation among the participants.

A second important role of the evaluation of PROMESA has been as a component in programme planning, through a system of evaluation-planning-action-evaluation-replanning-and-action. Formal evaluation based on initial objectives ignores the fact that a project will be faced with a series of other factors which will intervene in its progress, changing to an extent these initial objectives and the activities used to achieve them. As such an on-going process of evaluation and monitoring is essential to ensure that project planning is appropriate.

Nevertheless, while this dual purpose to evaluation has been central throughout PROMESA, the programme's directors were aware that using exclusively qualitative evaluation of this nature it is possible to mislead anyone you want to mislead, and while it is natural to want to look good in the eyes of the public, there is a real danger in misleading one's self. Moreover, the reality is such that social projects of this nature continue to need the financial support of national and international funders, and consequently there is a clear need for formal hard data to make a judgement of the relationship between observed outcomes and expected outcomes. For this reason, the evaluation of PROMESA has included a more formal component of evaluation, to analyse in a systematic way the accomplishment of initial objectives.

Evaluation as an On-Going Strategy for Reflection and Motivation

Monitoring or on-going evaluation play an important role in all the different programmes that form part of Project PROMESA. But more than merely monitoring, self-evaluation has been at the heart of this process. This type of monitoring and evaluation is done at all levels: with the mothers and community members; with the *promotoras*; with CINDE's field staff; and even to an extent with the project director.

This process of self-evaluation is done through various approaches, including:

(i) Reporting and Recording

At every meeting and event, a limited amount of data is recorded. This is done through two approaches. One is through an individual group record or some form of log-book. For example, at the meetings with pre-school mothers a point is made of evaluating the work done by each mother since the last encounter and how it has affected the development of her children. In the nutrition programme, the children are weighed and measured each week and a simple graph is developed by the mothers so that they can see the progress made. In the malaria programme, the *promotoras* who take the blood samples plot the cases of malaria and the types of malaria in this way, maintaining a clear record of the increases and decreases in the disease. Periodically, the group discusses the records reflecting on why there has be an improvement or decline in the results.

The second approach are the reports on activities written both by the *promotoras* and CINDE's field staff. In these reports the individuals note their observations with regards to the objectives, achievements and difficulties.

(ii) Survey / Diagnosis / Questionnaire

Generally, at the start of each programme or campaign, a survey has been done by the community to evaluate the situation. The most common approach used in PROMESA has been the design of a 'croquis' or three-dimensional map in which the community, based on the information which they collect using a survey or questionnaire, visually describe the problem. For instance, at the start of the campaign for the installation of latrines the community developed a map, locating the houses with latrines and those without latrines, and showing the altitude of the different parts of the community to indicate the possibility of underground septic tanks. This helps stimulate the community to visualise the problem, locating the areas where the problem is more severe, and creates a basis against which to evaluate their progress.

(iii) Group Discussions

The meetings and activities themselves are also evaluated through group discussions. Group discussions have been an important aspect throughout the programme. They provide an opportunity to discuss the collective views on the activities, the changes that seem to be occurring and for understanding in greater detail the quality of those changes.

(iv) Key Informants

Individual discussions with one or two *promotoras* or community leaders are also used in PROMESA as a way of monitoring developments and of checking the validity of previous findings.

(v) Workshops

At least once a year, workshops are organised with the *promotoras* and CINDE's staff to analyse developments, to check that the project is on course, and to make necessary changes.

All these different approaches serve to help the community reflect and visualise their problem and to stimulate and motivate them to continue with activities or to develop new actions. Moreover they serve as a form of continuous evaluation of project activities.

Evaluation for Programme Planning

A project usually begins by defining, together with the community, a set of objectives and strategies for achieving these objectives. What is normally assumed is that if there is a logical relationship between the objectives and the strategies planned, then the success of a project will depend on the extent to which these activities are implemented. As such, evaluation generally emphasises these initial objectives. In reality however, a project will be faced with a series of other factors that will intervene in its progress.

Take the example of a sailing boat. You have your goal or port clearly defined and you know how you are going to sail to get there, however, you must take into account the wind and you must tack and change your course as the wind changes. You will also be affected by the tides; at one time, the tide will be helping you, at another it will be impeding your progress. Furthermore, there are currents to contend with that will push you off course. Clearly then you will need to make changes as the 'forces' change. The same is true of a project, requiring a certain level of flexibility in terms of project planning. In project PROMESA, evaluation has played a central role in this process of planning-action-evaluation-replanning-and-action, which CINDE has referred to as the 'forces instrument'.

When PROMESA first began, a list was made of the major factors which had an impact on the project's progress. At this time, they included: CINDE's team, the local nuns with whom the project began, the promotoras, the training materials, the attitude of the local people, travel to the project area, local travel, communications, the educational level of the people, the local government, the climate, and malaria.

Having outlined the forces, values were assigned to them according to their relative strength or importance. For example, at the beginning the relative strengths of the different forces were interpreted as the following:

CINDE's team	20%
The local nuns	20%
Training materials	15%
Travel to the project	10%
Local travel	10%
Communications	10%
Education of the people	5%
Attitude of the people	5%
Local government	0%
Climate and malaria	5%

Having decided on the strength of the forces, each force was assigned a direction by creating a scale from (+)3 to (-)3. If the force was completely positive, we assigned a (+)3, if it was completely negative we assigned a (-)3.

At the start of PROMESA, CINDE's team was viewed as a positive force, although to begin with there were only two field workers, so there was a need to recruit and train others. As such, the team were assigned a force of (+)1. Initially the nuns were a very positive force in the programme; they represented a group of enthusiastic workers, their mission offered a place for CINDE's staff to stay and hold meetings, and their presence helped to encourage the local people to come to the meetings. At this stage, therefore, they were assigned a value of (+)3. Training materials were extremely important, but were non-existent at the time so the direction was negative (-)3.

Travel to the project was in an old aeroplane which, according to the weather and the plane's state of maintenance, flew three times a week. So this was an important but negative force hindering the project and was given (-)3. Once the field workers arrived at the project area, local travel was by water, using a dug out tree for a boat and an unreliable motor which slowed our movements and made our trips dependent on the flow of the tide and was given (-)3. Similarly, communications from CINDE's offices in Medellín to the project were almost non-existent. There was only one telephone in Bahía Solano, the largest community, but there was no means of communicating with the other three villages, Valle, Panguí and Nuquí and was given (-)3.

Clearly, the fact that 60-70% of the local population could not read or write created a problem and was given (-)3. But the attitude of the people was very positive and this helped to counteract their lack of education and was given (+)3. Moreover although the local government would probably become a force in the near future, at this initial stage of the project it was neither a positive nor a negative force and was given 0.

Finally the climate and malaria were other factors which we had to consider in our plans. CINDE's team was not accustomed to the climate and the medicine available to prevent malaria was not effective and was given (-)3.

In order to develop a clearer picture of the relative importance of the different forces we multiplied the strength by the direction (see Table 3.2). These forces were then analysed with the team and the *promotoras*. Through this process the group decided that before they could even start to achieve the original objectives something would have to be done to overcome these negative forces.

Table 3.2
Forces and Directions of the PROMESA Programme

FORCES	STRENGTH	DIRECTION	COMBINED EFFORT
CINDE's team	20%	+1	+20
Local Nuns	20%	+1	+60
Training Materials	15%	−3	−45
Travel to Project	10%	−3	−30
Local Travel	10%	−3	−30
Communication	10%	−3	−30
People's Education	5%	−3	−15
People's Attitude	5%	+3	+15
Local Government	0%	0	0
Climate and Malaria	5%	−3	−15

The decisions therefore were:

(i) To strengthen CINDE's team by recruiting and training three Colombian professionals, and appointing one of the nuns as field director.

(ii) To develop materials as a part of the training of new staff.

(iii) To ask for a permit to use a radio-telephone in order to communicate with the villages.

(iv) To write to the van Leer Foundation asking them to advance the money which had been specified in the budget for the rent of a boat for three years, so that the project could buy its own boat and motor.

(v) To initiate a campaign against malaria, which involved: education in the production and use of mosquito nets; training for paramedics in the extraction and analysis of blood samples, in order to prescribe appropriate medicine for the different types of malaria; organisation of the local communities to drain away stagnant waters where the mosquitos lay their larvae; and the implementation of a programme for the biological control of malaria.

These decisions were put into effect and a year later the forces analysis was applied again. Based on the new interpretation of the forces the planning policy for the next year was developed. This strategy continued to be carried out on a yearly basis, and slowly changes were made. For example, over time the nuns changed from being a strong positive force, to that of a negative force while on the contrary the *promotoras* became more positive, and consequently a decision was made to slowly withdraw the nuns from the programme and to let the local *promotoras* fill this role.

The forces instrument shows therefore how periodic evaluations in Project PROMESA have been used as an important factor in the process of flexible and participatory planning and activities.

Evaluation of Initial Objectives

All the qualitative evaluations described above have been done as an integral part of project development. In addition a series of evaluations of impact have been carried out systematically over the years to judge the accomplishments with regards to the intellectual and physical development of children and the self-concept of their parents. The objective here has been to determine to what degree Project PROMESA has helped to improve the health, local environment and educational level of the schools, and to what degree it has 'empowered' the communities to achieve this. This evaluation was done through a series of questionnaires, informal discussions and educational tests applied to the children, their mothers, and the *promotoras*. The following is a summary of the major findings of the quantitative evaluations between 1980 and 1992.

Evaluating the Impact of PROMESA on the Physical Development of the Children

PROMESA's efforts to improve the healthy physical development of the children of Choco, have involved working in two principal areas:

(i) Providing primary health care services;

(ii) Using relevant technology to improve the local environment where children live.

Consequently, the evaluation of the physical development of the children and their mothers involved: (1) reporting on the process of providing primary health care; (2) evaluating improvements in the sanitary conditions within the communities; and, (3) looking at the combined effects of those two programmes on the health of the children and mothers.

The primary health care programme has consisted of training local women to serve as paramedics. Despite the very low level of literacy of these women, they have learned to give first aid, take blood pressure, use a microscope to diagnose malaria, recognise common illnesses and treat them. Also they learned to conduct neighbourhood meetings to discuss health problems such as sanitation in the house, the need for dental care, good water and clean streets and beaches. Additionally, the primary health care programme has formed the base for the 'flying doctors' programme, in which young doctors and interns come to the community once a month to examine those people with more serious problems.

Moreover, as well as learning to diagnose for malaria and other minor illnesses, the *promotoras* also learned to give vaccinations. Through their efforts, and a government programme, the number of people who have been vaccinated has increased. For example, the percentage of children who had received one or more of the desirable vaccinations in 1980 was 46%, by 1986 that figure had increased to 72%, and by 1989 it had reached 95%. Although the federal government conducted a national campaign for vaccinations in 1985 and 1986, this programme would not have reached the people of Chocó without the help of the primary health care programme. It was the *promotoras* who provided the transportation and lodgings for the doctors and nurses, and they were the ones who organised the campaign within the region.

Efforts to improve the local environment have had mixed results. A campaign for the installation of latrines, has meant that some of the communities have gone from having no latrines to almost 100%, whilst others have gone from almost none to 50%, the exemption being Pangui, where still only 6% of the houses have latrines. Availability of drinking water has also been improved in two of the four original communities but there has been little progress in the others. The problem of garbage, on the streets and beaches has however substantially improved in three of the four communities, and stagnant water, where mosquitoes breed, has been drained away in some places.

Thus for the most part the primary health care programme was effective, while efforts to improve the physical environment have been more or less successful. The real question, however, is whether the project has made an observable impact on the health of the people. To evaluate this we looked at the number of pregnancies, miscarriages, still births and live births in 1980, 1986 and 1989. The graph on the next page summarises the mortality rates for 1980 and 1989. The deaths per 1,000 during the first five years of life were 117 in 1980, and 76 in 1989, or in other words the mortality rate in these communities had fallen from being one of the highest in Colombia, to being close to the national average and on par with the average for all of South and Central America. Between 1980 and 1989 the average mortality rate for Colombia has decreased by 1.74 per year; in Chocó it has decreased by 3.7 per year, or in other words twice as fast.

Consequently, one of the conclusions reached from the evaluation has been that although not all of the improvements in health and sanitary conditions can be attributed to PROMESA (the government programme of vaccination and the increase in the number of tourists visiting the region also had an impact), the project did serve as a catalyst for many of the improvements, and the final outcome was in this way greater than its input.

Evaluating the Impact of PROMESA on the Intellectual Development of the Children

One of the focuses of the evaluation was the educational achievement of the children, since it was reasoned that if the children were staying in school longer and achieving more, then it could be assumed that:

(i) The *promotoras* had been successful in helping the mothers learn to stimulate the intellectual development of their pre-school children.

(ii) The mothers had not only learned how to use the materials, but they had taken the time to use them with their children.

Furthermore, in addition to these two principle assumptions, it was presumed that enough mothers were involved in the programme to have an impact on the entire community, and that the educational climate had improved not only in the home, but in the schools and the community as well.

As such, there were two questions which the evaluation needed to answer: (i) are children staying in school longer?; (ii) are they learning more than they did before and are these improvements being sustained over a number of years?

(i) Are the children staying in school longer?
The results of the evaluation to establish the grade level achieved by children of different ages, showed that in 1980 only 17% of twelve year olds had reached fifth grade, but by 1986 this number had risen to 51%, a clear indication therefore that children were staying in school longer. The next question which needed to be established, was whether this increase was the result of PROMESA's impact?

Children who were twelve years old in 1986 were young enough to have been involved in PROMESA's pre-school programme during the initial years of the project. Some fifteen year olds could possibly have been involved in the programme, but eighteen year olds clearly could not have been affected, as they would have been ten years old when PROMESA began in 1978 (and PROMESA was for children seven years or younger). The average grade level of twelve year old children in 1980 was 2.58, while by 1986 this average had risen to 3.55, or in other words a difference of a whole grade. In the meantime, during the same period the average grade level for the fifteen and eighteen year olds did not change, remaining at 4.7 and 6.0 respectively.

By 1989, some of the children who had been involved in PROMESA when the programme first begun, had reached the age of eighteen. Figure 3.2 shows the average grade achieved by children aged between eleven and twenty in 1989. It is clear from these results that the younger children are staying in school longer, since there is a difference of less than one grade between the fifteen year old children and the eighteen year olds. Moreover, 95% of the fifteen year olds were still in school in 1989, whereas only 50% of the eighteen year olds were, which means that by the time the present group of fifteen year olds reach eighteen their average grade level will be above that of the present group of eighteen year olds, and well above that of the nineteen and twenty year olds who could not possibly have participated in PROMESA. Thus the results show that during since PROMESA started, children are staying in school longer. For instance, if we look at the twelve year olds in 1980 and 1989, we see that their average grade level increased from 2.5 in 1980 to 4.2 in 1989.

(ii) Has the children's achievement improved?
To test whether the children's school achievement was improving, three related achievement tests were developed. The first was applied to both first and second grade children, the second was used for third grade children, and the third was applied to the fourth and fifth grade children. Each of these tests contained sub-tests on mathematics, language and problem solving.

In the evaluation of school achievement among children of Chocó, a 'cohort design' was used. That is to say, the children who were in first grade at the time the programme started, formed the comparison group for children who entered first grade one year later, and these children formed the comparison group for those one year younger than them, and so on. Using this method, it could be concluded that if PROMESA's parent-child programme was being effective in its aim of providing pre-school children more opportunities to learn, then each year the children in first grade should test somewhat better than those children who were in the first

88

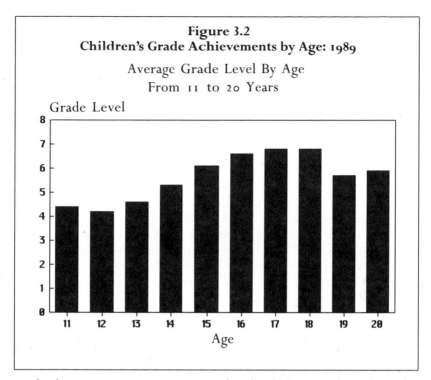

Figure 3.2
Children's Grade Achievements by Age: 1989

Average Grade Level By Age
From 11 to 20 Years

grade the previous year. Moreover, this should be true throughout the elementary grades as the project progressed and had an impact on a greater number of families and children. A cohort design was used because there was no way of forming a comparative group that would be similar enough to the children in PROMESA.

The results of the tests were as was predicted. The results obtained by the children of the following year were a little higher than those of the same age group the year before. Moreover, this pattern was the same for every grade level in all three of the tests: mathematics, language, and problem-solving. What is more, by 1985 the fourth grade children were testing as high or higher than the fifth grade children had tested in 1981, which in effect represents a gain of one school year.

The conclusions drawn from these results were that the children now are staying in school longer and doing better. This implies that:

(a) The *promotoras*, or local women, have been successful in helping mothers to learn how to educate their children in the home; or, in other words, they have been able to carry out a role which in most societies has been reserved for professional pre-school teachers or educators of parents. This is evidently true since the results were achieved without any member of CINDE's staff working directly with the mothers or children.

(b) The mothers have learned to play with their children, using educational games to develop the intellectual ability of the children.

Moreover, because the improvements are being sustained and are having an effect up into the fifth grade, we can assume there is a better climate for education in the home, barrio and community, than there was before the programme began.

Evaluating the Impact of PROMESA on the Process of Empowering the Families and Communities

From the project's perspective, enabling or 'empowering' the families and communities to attend to the needs of the healthy development of their young children, means ensuring that the people not only know what to do, but that they have the ability to do it. This implies that they must have self-confidence, be self-reliant, and they must have a feeling of being in control of many of the things that affect their lives. This has involved three aspects:

(i) Improving the vocational skills of the local people so that they can improve their economic standing, enabling them to buy some of the things required for their children's development

(ii) Improving the self-image and confidence of the local people so that they will attempt to overcome some of their problems

(iii) Educating a group of community leaders and *promotoras* with the organisational skills and confidence to create both informal and formal groups to promote community programmes and attend to the different problems that arise.

From the start of the project, it was reasoned that if parents become more self-confident of their ability to attend to the needs of their children, and if they become more self-reliant, then the chances of maintaining the gains in the physical and psychological development of the children, and improving upon these, will also increase. If on the other hand the gains are primarily the result of some outside intervention, they will stop when the intervention stops. Evaluating the self-image of the mothers was therefore a central part of the evaluation of PROMESA.

As such in 1977, 1980, 1985, 1989, and 1992, a series of questionnaires were applied to the parents and adults in the communities to evaluate their self-image, and their participation in vocational and parent education programmes. In terms of their participation in parent and vocational training courses, there was a marked increase. When PROMESA began, none of the parents had taken adult education courses, but by 1989, 80% had participated in one or more of the parent education programmes organised by the *promotoras* of PROMESA.

In terms of the confidence and self-image of the people, it was assumed that if these had increased then this would be reflected in:

(i) A feeling of being able to help the family, neighbourhood and community.

(ii) A belief that they can influence people in the family, neighbourhood and community.

(iii) A belief that they have control over the events that affect their lives and the lives of their children.

(iv) A belief that they are better able to meet the physical needs of their children.

The evaluation was particularly concerned with looking at the relationship between the parents' participation in the programme over the ten years, and their self-image and ability to attend to their children. As such the individuals interviewed were divided into four groups, according to how long and to what degree they had participated in the programme, and their responses to the following questions were analysed:

When you look back over the last ten years:

• are you better able to help your family now?

• are you better able to help the community?

• do you have more confidence in yourself?

• can you solve your personal problems better now than you could before?

• when you propose some ideas to improve the family, the barrio and the community, are your ideas accepted in the family, in the barrio and in the community?

In most interviews, people tend to tell the interviewer what they think the interviewer wants to hear and this probably occurred to some extent. Nevertheless, on every question the pattern was the same; the mothers with the least participation had the lowest average score and the mothers with the highest participation had the highest average score.

Further evidence that the level of self-confidence and self-reliance of the people has increased comes from the fact that they have organised themselves legally to improve both their own and their community's physical and economic conditions. And, at one stage when the financing for the project ended several years ago, the *promotoras* concluded that they were the most important outcome of the project, stating that 'we need your help, but we can continue without you'. The project has been continuing ever since, and new ways to cope with the emerging problems have been found. That is the best evaluation that the project could ever possibly have received.

Conclusion

The goal of PROMESA has been to improve the environment for the healthy physical and psychological development of young children. The means of achieving this goal has been to enable or 'empower' the families and communities to achieve this through the development of a flexible and participatory programme. Evaluation within PROMESA has consequently played a number of roles. On the one hand, it has helped the local people through a process of self-evaluation to become aware that they are able to do something to change their situation and to improve the lives of their children. On the other hand, evaluation has played an important role in the flexible planning of activities, and in ensuring that activities and decisions respond to needs. Finally, through a more formal evaluation of the impact of PROMESA, it has been possible to demonstrate to funders and government bodies the value of family and community based programmes for the healthy development of young children.

Group Discussion on the PROMESA Case Study

There was a great deal of interest in the example of PROMESA given that it was a genuine attempt to maintain an evaluative system of a social development programme over more than a decade. Some of the key areas which emerged include the following:

Evaluation as part of the process: It is interesting to note that CINDE made a very clear and unequivocal statement on evaluation:

Evaluation is a part of the social development process since it is inherent in the educational process implied therein. It depends on, and strengthens, community organisation and is indispensable to building local capacity for self determination, self direction and hence self-reliance on the part of the community.

Therefore, it is not surprising that we discovered that evaluation is carried out at all levels of the programme. This started with the individual evaluation of participants own performance, and personal plans and growth, through to more elaborate evaluations of major sectoral aspects of the programme (e.g. malaria control etc.).

Identification of different perceptions: The case study dwelt on the necessity of ensuring that all the different participants in the programme are assisted in clarifying and articulating their own perceptions of the programme and the development process. Elsewhere we have talked about the identification of stakeholder interests; here the programme recognised not only the need to identify interests, but also different perceptions. We were told that different strategies and methods were required for different types of participants to develop their own criteria and indicators regarding the development process in which they were engaged. It was explained that everyone should be involved; children, parents, staff, through to the CINDE advisers to PROMESA, using methodologies appropriate to each group.

Two way accountability: There was considerable discussion about the way in which all participants in the programme were able to become involved in evaluating the programme itself. Thus while the *promotoras* evaluated the performance of their community groups, these groups themselves made evaluations of their *promotoras*. This was regarded as still relatively unusual. We were further intrigued to discover that occasionally *promotoras* had been removed due to negative evaluations from communities. Our interest was even more aroused when it was explained that the *promotoras* in turn evaluated their supervisors and vice versa, and that occasionally this had also led to staff changes. This process of two way evaluation continued throughout the complete system, including the advisory group of CINDE.

Permanent record keeping: Some people were concerned by the apparently high burden imposed by a system which seemed to imply a perhaps onerous degree of record keeping, and possibly the accumulation of a great deal of paper at all levels. For instance, each individual was encouraged to keep a personal record of their plans and achievements, whether they are a member of a 'mothers group' or of the staff. Minutes were taken at all the meetings of the community groups, the evaluation sessions were recorded and so on. It was not clear how much time this actually absorbed in addition to the act of discussing issues of concern to the groups. However, it was recognised that these records improved transparency, and facilitated the occasional traditional external evaluation carried out by CINDE. These were conducted to cross check on the self evaluation process and for the purpose of learning from the experience of the programme for the benefit of other such programmes.

In addition, several other points emerged:

• this type of self evaluation does sometimes require cross checking through other means, especially where more traditional quantative data is required (e.g. on health indices etc.);

• donors have often been reluctant to meet the costs of such evaluation processes. We were unable to compare the relative costs of this system to other more traditional evaluations;

• a major lesson to come from this case study was that evaluation must meet the needs of all the participants at all levels, in this case from the children to the foreign donors;

• there should be a strong educational element in the evaluation process;

• often organisations have difficulties in seeing evaluation as a part of their history and as opportunities for learning and improvement.

CHAPTER FOUR

APPROACHES TO EVALUATING SOCIAL DEVELOPMENT

'Indicators and Methodologies Cannot Replace Common Sense' (Anon)

Introduction

In the context of the above words of wisdom, the first major activity of the Workshop was a detailed examination of the approaches to the evaluation of social development used by the different written case studies. In the preparation of these studies a protocol had been designed and used as the basis for structuring material into a comparable case study format. On reflection, this proved a useful way of giving some common structure to what were a diverse set of studies. In the different studies, evaluation approaches ranged from highly participatory, using innovative techniques of information gathering and analysis, to the more conventional, quantitative approaches in which 'beneficiaries' had only limited involvement. Without a predetermined structure of presentation, it might well have proved impossible to compare the different studies. In all nine studies were presented from Peru, Colombia, Zimbabwe (2), Ethiopia, Mali (2) and India (2). Inevitably the nine studies had interpreted the case study protocol in their own particular styles, but the end result was a set of documents which could be used for comparative purposes.

Two immediate observations made on the case studies were as follows. First, that a fundamental first step is to determine and to be sure that 'we know where we are coming from'. In other words, that a project has a firm and clear understanding of what it means by 'social development' and that it is consistent in this understanding. This observation, of course, opens up a whole area of literature and statements on social development which can be found both in the study on the earlier workshop and in the literature review in Chapter 2; it is, however, critical to reinforce it here and to continue to hammer home the point that a consistent and transparent interpretation of social development is the basic first element without which any evaluation is doomed before it starts. Second, that in the evaluation of social development it is equally critical not to approach the evaluation as if it were a discrete exercise. The evaluation of social development does not only deal with the details of the programme or project; equally it is concerned with the structural factors which can influence the outcome of such projects. Evaluation is a critical element in the whole process of social development and not merely a one-off activity to temporarily assess the actual outcome. This outcome can never be understood as a 'snap-shot' view at any one moment in the project's development; it must be seen as continually evolving, and even changing, and its evaluation needs to be sensitive to this fact.

Since the majority of participants attending the workshop represented donor agencies, inevitably opening comments were made concerning donor's attitudes to the evaluation of social development projects. In general terms, it was felt that Northern donor agencies had still not yet come to terms with a more process, as opposed to an end-product, approach to social development evaluation. While paying lip-service to the former, agencies' headquarters in particular were still largely dominated by the latter. The result was that currently donor agencies were still more concerned with gathering lots of quantitative data and information in a one-off exercise and were still not at ease with an approach to evaluation which did not necessarily have such neat boundaries. Similarly, at both the headquarters and project level, there was much written commitment to the notion of evaluation as a participatory exercise, but the reality was that few such projects adopted an authentic participatory approach to evaluation. A major stumbling block to more innovative approaches to evaluation was still the blinkered view of donor agencies that evaluation is essentially to do with justifying expenditure.

In this more generalised open debate on the evaluation of social development a series of other important issues were raised: for example, the question of the mix of different methodologies, both quantitative and qualitative, or whether social development evaluation demanded a more rigid set of pre-determined methods; the issue of rigour and the importance of ensuring that the methodologies selected would ensure a rigorous and 'scientifically' based approach to the evaluation; the continual dilemma of 'internal' versus 'external' and what was an appropriate balance between beneficiary participation and external consultancy in these evaluations; the importance of recognising that evaluation demanded a set of particular skills on the part of those involved and that it should not be assumed that all professionals were equally competent to undertake one; and the growing importance of the need to keep an eye on the costs of social development evaluation and to submit even the most participatory approaches to some notion of cost-effectiveness. Finally it was recognised that there was an 'ethical' dimension to all evaluation activities—'we are messing around with peoples' lives'—but, while it was often in the air, this dimension rarely broke the surface. In terms of some of these more general issues or questions raised concerning the evaluation of social development the following six questions form GEAP, Mali, are illustrative, although it must be recognised that such questions are appropriate to most evaluation work.

Box 4.1
Six Questions to Ask about
Social Development Evaluation

(1)   For whom is the Evaluation?
(2)   For what purpose is the Evaluation?
(3)   What will be the objectives of the Evaluation?
(4)   According to what will we evaluate the results?
(5)   Who evaluates whom?
(6)   When do we evaluate an action?

(GEAP, Mali)

Frameworks of Approach

An important and critical first stage in any social development evaluation is to do with establishing a framework as a basic guide to implementing the evaluation. Such a framework acts as a kind of overall reference for the whole exercise and is often built around a series of principles or critical elements which establish the basis upon which the evaluation will be carried out. It is the case that not all such evaluations refer explicitly to a 'framework' as such, but increasingly social development evaluations are based upon some kind of construct which helps determine and guide implementation. An evaluation 'framework', of course, has a direct bearing upon the evaluation approach and, it could be argued, it is indispensable in social development. Evaluations without this kind of framework can become ad-hoc, simple data collection exercises in order to try to present the quantitative project outcome; in social development such an approach would fail to grasp the complex and partly qualitative nature of such outcomes. It could be argued, therefore, that unless it is undertaken on the basis of a carefully prepared framework of interpretation and operational principles, any social development evaluation will be reduced to the snap-shot collection of quantifiable data.

However, in the evaluation of social development there is no such thing as a common framework. Unlike what we tend to call the 'conventional approach' to evaluation, the evaluation of social development has few core elements. For example, it could be argued that 'conventional approaches' to evaluation tend to have the following core elements; desk study, document content analysis, quantitative survey, analysis of results and written report. Similarly such evaluations tend to be externally led and to be concerned almost exclusively with the tangible aspects of project outcome. In comparison, approaches to the evaluation of social development employ such terms as 'participatory evaluation', 'auto-evaluation', 'qualitative evaluation' and 'alternative evaluation', and are approaches to evaluation which tend to be stronger on principles than on techniques. Furthermore training in a more conventional, quantitative approach to evaluation is predicated on the assumption that the crucial task is to teach the evaluators a set of common skills; whereas involvement in social development evaluations stresses the importance of approach and of translating the principles of the approach into the context of the project.

One important dimension of evaluation which can help illustrate the issue of approach is to do with the relative balance between the qualitative and quantitative aspects of social development evaluation. We have seen this matter addressed in some detail in the Zimbabwe case study above, which sought from the outset to achieve some kind of balance and which would appear to have had some success. While other studies (Peru, Colombia and India, for example) touched upon the issue and argued that both aspects were important, few raised this issue of balance. Since conventional evaluations tend to be almost wholly quantitative, could it be argued that social development evaluation should be wholly qualitative? Furthermore, is it possible, as some would argue, to quantify the qualitative outcomes of social development? The answer would appear to be 'yes'; the danger is that many social development projects overlook the issue of balance and seek to put a numerical value on all aspects of social development projects.

In examining the different case studies presented to the workshop, we can note a number of examples of the overall framework for the evaluation of social development projects. The following are several brief examples of such evaluation frameworks:

(i) Prajwala, India
In this case study two broad types of evaluation are identified:

(a) *OEP: On going Evaluation Process*. This is an internal process whereby the team of Prajwala comes together to reflect upon, guide and plan its work in social development. Major shifts in programmes and direction in Prajwala and an assessment of current problems and advances are decided upon after on OEP exercise. The OEP is a crucial, continuous evaluation process which helps both to check the relevance of the intervention and to determine and identify emerging outcomes.

(b) *TEE: Time-Bound Evaluation Exercise.* Such exercises are usually carried out by external resource persons and take a particular point in time as the cut-off time and reflects back on the whole process that proceeded it.

Prajwala uses these two frameworks of evaluation both individually and jointly. Furthermore it sees the role of TEE as essentially to check the OEP and validate it. With the help and expertise of external consultants it is possible to objectively assess the OEP and recommend appropriate new directions. OEP and TEE are, therefore, two sides of the same coin. TEE is useful in periodically counter-checking OEP, and yet TEE is meaningless unless supported by regular OEP.

(ii) Groupe d'Appui aux Projects: MALI
This project has developed an approach which uses techniques of animation to develop a process of self-evaluation in social development. The process is developed in three stages and it is the latter stage that is crucial for developing the idea of self-evaluation:

Creating: The animator helps the member of the group to become aware of their own situation and to recognise the importance of taking responsibilities for their development in their own hands.

Realisation: The animator helps the group to plan and to realise an action which would help to improve the situation of the community.

Scrutinisation: The animator helps the members of the group to think about the importance of the activity they undertook in terms of the daily life of the community and to create an inner dynamic in the group leading to further development.

The Mali project confirmed that self-evaluation is a time consuming process and that it can take up to 10–15% of project time. Consistency is crucial to the process and self-evaluation fails in many projects due to frequent changes both in project direction and staff.

(iii) CEAR: Brazil
In CEAR's practice with social development evaluation with a range of NGOs and base groups in Brazil, the distinction is drawn between two broad frameworks:

Formative Evaluation: Which develops a framework of evaluation based upon different forms and evaluation needs. The forms range from the regular community praxis of planning, acting, evaluating and replanning, to the more one-off exercises such as annual reports. An essential ingredient of these different forms is that they are seen as educational and as part of the overall development of the activity.

Summative Evaluation: Which is more concerned with building a coherent and planned approach to evaluation based on a number of pre-determined elements; e.g. context diagnosis, stabilising of value position, judgement, analysis and evaluation.

The essential difference between the two frameworks is that the former incorporates a whole series of on-going process, while the latter is a more structured, almost one-off activity. Both have their place in social development evaluation and yet both demand different personnel and techniques.

Apart from the above overall frameworks relating to particular social development projects, there were a number of more common 'framework' elements which were noted in different case studies. If we summarise these, then the more important ones were as follows:

Simple versus sophisticated approach: There would appear to be evidence of social development projects, which for years perhaps had gone un-evaluated, suddenly being thrust by a concerned agency into the complex and sophisticated world of social development evaluation. Such odd and eccentric approaches can often lead to bewilderment on the part of project staff and unreality in terms of expectations for a sudden reversal of established evaluation practice. Beware of the animator decked out with all the modern jargon of evaluation on a project which has lain peaceful but progressing for a decade or so.

The use of the counterfactual: What is the utility of 'control groups' in the evaluation of social development and how far should their use be a basic principle of operation? There is an ethical dimension to the use of control groups and yet there is a lot of evidence of their usefulness in the evaluation process.

An 'imposed' versus an 'owned' approach: This contrast is at the heart of social development evaluation. The determination of whether the exercise will either be essentially 'imposed' from outside or 'owned' by project participants will colour the whole process and will be the overriding influence in its implementation.

The cost of evaluation: This issue rightly came to the surface. It would appear that little work to date has been done either on the issue of the economic cost of social development projects or on the costs of the evaluation of these projects. Techniques such as group discussions, workshops, longitudinal studies and regular monitoring, are all potentially costly. Yet the issue of the costs of such evaluations has not to date seemed to have figured widely in discussions on social development evaluation.

A further way of examining the issues of overall approaches in the evaluation of social development and the often contrasting elements in different approaches can be seen in Box 4.2 which has been constructed on the basis the different case studies presented to the Workshop. This Box suggests the more important elements in the evaluation of social development. They are not presented in any way as a definitive set of elements but more as yet another illustration of the issue of approaches and elements.

The purpose of this section has not been to construct a model framework of approach to the evaluation of social development; rather the purpose has been to underline and to emphasise the importance of such a framework as fundamental to any exercise of social development evaluation. The focus of the section has been eclectic, drawing upon a variety of examples from different sources in order to illustrate the matter as widely as possible. Furthermore in this section a purpose has been to argue that without even some loosely constructed framework of approach, a social development evaluation can degenerate into a series of disjointed and unrelated activities. During the process of a social development evaluation, decisions will need to be constantly made; without any overall framework of approach, such decisions might be clutching at thin air. Unlike more conventional and quantitative evaluation, social development evaluation does not enjoy the luxury of limited vision and expected outcome.

Key Stages in Evaluation Approaches

As a way of giving coherence to a potentially heterogeneous collection of case studies, a protocol was prepared which suggested that the overall process of social development evaluation could be seen as a series of stages. Case study presenters, therefore, were asked to reflect upon the process as a whole and, where feasible, to structure the material on the basis of these stages: preparation, execution, reporting and analysis. The three studies presented in Chapter 3 illustrate how this approach was used; the other studies examined at the Workshop also largely followed this structure. The stages were not selected arbitrarily nor are they relevant

---

Box 4.2
Important Elements in the
Evaluation of Social Development

(a) Self–Evaluation: Professional Evaluation
The importance of balance between two valid approaches.

(b) History: Memory
Often forgotten elements in evaluation. If the history or memory of a project are limited or non-existent, then a formal evaluation will be necessary. Much of the history or memory of a project are often lost in disorganised files or in staffs' heads and are unable to contribute to evaluation.

(c) Mixture: Creativity
In any evaluation exercise, a mix of methods and techniques is more creative; a major stumbling block with many NGO evaluations, however, is how to encourage creativity in the evaluation process as opposed to the automatic resort to controlled quantitative methods.

(d) Choice: Interest
Who decides upon the approach to an evaluation and in whose interest is the approach decided? In any evaluation exercise, different interests will be involved and it will be important to note who makes the choice.

(e) Participation: Democracy
Participation might be an overall aim of an evaluation exercise but it must be understood in relation to the situation of 'democracy' within the country concerned. Too many evaluations have overlooked this relationship between participation in evaluation and levels of democratic involvement with the country as a whole.

---

only to the evaluation of social development; they are clearly recognisable 'stages' of any evaluation exercise which has been thought out and is conducted in a structured fashion. The following is a discussion and analysis of both the different case study materials and the Workshop group sessions around these four key stages of the overall social development evaluation process. Essentially it is a summary of the main findings around each stage; a more detailed description of each stage can be seen in each of the three case studies in Chapter 3.

I. Preparation

This is the critical first stage when essentially the central framework of the evaluation is constructed. Several projects referred to the notion of a pre-preparation phase; this is a phase when such questions as 'why?' or the reasons for the evaluation are openly articulated and when the more general concerns, on the basis of which objectives will be formulated, are aired. This preparation phase similarly might raise questions such as 'who takes the initiative?' or 'who poses the initial questions?' Clearly this preparation period is important for asking those 'ethical' or 'ideological' questions which it would be too late to ask once the exercise begins. Such questions are crucial in laying down the very 'core' or 'thrust' of the evaluation and will prove fundamental in determining how and on what basis the evaluation exercise will be developed. How long such a pre-preparation period might take or who might be involved is open to question; it would appear, however, that in some case studies (Peru, Zimbabwe and India) there had been lengthy discussions around these and other questions a considerable time before the exercise evaluation began, both at the donor agency and project partner levels.

A more substantial examination of the different case studies suggests four key aspects of the preparation stage. Each of these is presented below:

(1) Objectives
In this respect we refer to the objectives of the evaluation and not necessarily the objectives of the social development project being evaluated, although we would expect that there is a direct relationship between the both. Overall, in their introductions the studies were surprisingly weak in identifying and explaining the objectives of social development, and this inevitably resulted in a lack of clarity and, in some cases, even detail as to the objectives of the evaluation exercise. In several instances there was even an apparent lack of consistency between an expressed interpretation of social development and the objectives of the evaluation exercise. More generally in the studies there was a heavy reliance upon objectives which could be more easily quantified and a suggestion that the objectives agreed reflected more the interest of the external donors and not necessarily the project participants. For example, it was not always clear who had been involved in the formulation of the objectives nor how they had been formulated. While most of the studies were emphatic that the determining of the objectives was a key first step, nonetheless in many cases there was little evidence that this had been done in a manner consistent with their expressed understanding of social development. It was difficult to avoid the conclusion that this step in the exercise had been completed with only limited consultation and with resort

to more quickly identifiable quantitative objectives.

(2) Terms of Reference (TOR)

The extent to which the studies were essentially orientated towards external concerns and were less a product of internal discussion and agreement is reflected in the formality of the TOR, which were a feature of most of the evaluations. The TOR of the different evaluation exercises ranged from: (i) a highly structured, sample-survey approach in which methods and checklists to be used were spelt out (India); (ii) a less rigid set of TOR, which included scope for the holding of seminars and instructions to consult with local people (Zimbabwe); (iii) a much more open approach in which the TOR were almost deliberately vague and where the different actors were encouraged to develop both methods and direction as the evaluation unfolded (Mali). TOR are a product of a particular approach to evaluation. They formalise and put boundaries around the process; while clearly some notion of direction and expected content and approach of an evaluation are critical, the building of these elements in pre-determined TOR leaves less room for developing the evaluation exercise as it unfolds. Indeed it could be argued that it would be surprising to find such a thing as TOR in the evaluation of social development. TOR are essentially both an external construct and, rightly or wrongly, heavily identified with a less-participatory and more one-off quantitative approach to evaluation. While the concept of some kind of formal 'guide' is probably appropriate to any kind of evaluation exercise, it would appear that such a task still remains for the evaluation of social development; hence the current resort to formal TOR.

(3) Data and Information

It is a fact both that appropriate data and information are crucial inputs into any evaluation exercise and also that many such exercises are launched from poor data and information bases. While most of the studies stressed the importance of data and information, most similarly reported either a non-existent or an inadequate data base prior to the evaluation beginning. Several studies (Zimbabwe and Mali) also reported little information upon the 'vision' of the project, its underlying basic purpose and its understanding of social development. In such instances evaluations are based on what one can find; initial situation analysis, survey records, minutes of meetings, field reports, supporting studies, financial statements and so on. None of the studies addressed the issue of the kinds of information and data more appropriate to the evaluation of social development, nor the forms that this data and information could take. This lack of a widening of the debate on what constitutes relevant data and information is very much a reflection of the 'external' orientation of the evaluation exercises, where data and information are defined in terms of those which are readily accessible and 'evaluator-friendly'. The issue is particularly complicated in respect to social development evaluation. As the case studies confirmed, evaluation studies in general are plagued by a chronic lack of timely, appropriate and accessible quantitative data. When we now turn to the same issue in the context of the qualitative information needed in the evaluation of social development, we can probably appreciate the magnitude of the problem.

(4) Evaluation Team

The concept of the 'team' is quite common in evaluation exercises. While, however, in most of the studies the notion of a 'resource person(s)' or some body of people responsible for guiding the evaluation exercise was evident, in a few this was formalised around the idea of a team. On review it was noted that, among the disciplines, economists and social anthropologists were thicker on the ground; community development workers were also referred to, as were team members who were representatives of the donor organisation. The studies, however, are somewhat sparse on such detail as how the composition of the team was determined, what were the expected skills and areas of knowledge around which the team was put together and how was the role and functioning of the team conceptualised. In the circumstances, it was difficult not to form the image of a somewhat divorced and independent body of people drawing upon local knowledge and information but not actually sharing the experience directly with project participants.

During this preparatory stage it is also useful to assess the expectations which the different actors may have of the evaluation exercise. Inevitably the potential actors—donor agency, development agency, project staff and participants—may well take different views of such things on the purpose of the evaluation, the roles of the different actors and the uses to which the results will be put. It would be remarkable if absolute harmony could be achieved around these different issues. However, during preparation it will be critical to cement whatever harmony is achievable and not move into execution without a broad body of support for and understanding by all the actors of the evaluation about to take place.

II. Execution

A general principle to be followed in the execution of a social development evaluation is that for different situations and contexts there will be a similarly different range of methods which will be appropriate. While rigour is important in the sense of seeking to achieve an outcome which has some 'scientific' basis, equally important will be 'mix' or the adaptation of the appropriate techniques to the given situation. Each of the case studies gave evidence of the notion of 'mix', even if essentially they divided into two broad approaches to evaluation in terms of its execution: (i) the more classical and formal survey/questionnaire/interview schedule approach; and (ii) the more Freirian type of evaluation methodology, with its accompanying elements of discussion, identification, reflection and analysis. A central principle of execution running through all the case studies, however, was the inevitable notion of 'participation'; this was seen as the essential 'philosophy' of execution but, understandably, the nature of its implementation was very much a function of the overall style of execution. To participate in providing information for a questionnaire survey could be said to be very different than participating in analysing and determining, in open discussions, the outcome of a project.

The three case studies in Chapter 3 above show us the detail of this particular stage of the evaluation process. Building upon these, and examination of the case study materials, suggested the following as two key elements in this stage of the evaluation process:

(i) The Evaluation Workplan

We have seen above in the Zimbabwe Case Study in Chapter 3 an example of a detailed workplan over a 12 month period, from the moment of the approval of the terms of reference to the formal presentation of the evaluation results at national level. Given the complex and extensive nature of the work of the Catholic Development Commission, the substantial resources made available for the evaluation and the 'national' expectation of the results, such a structured workplan can be understood. However, few of the studies elevated this aspect of the evaluation to the notion of a workplan in the formal sense; most preferred a much looser understanding of the parameters of the evaluation activities. Generally, in the case studies there was concern to define a clear period of work for the evaluation, to allow sufficient time for the evaluation to take place, to set targets at particular stages in order to structure the work and to conclude the period of the evaluation with some kind of formal reporting. An exception was the evaluation of the Water Project in Mali which was spread over such a long period of time (two and a half years) that expatriate staff changes and normal internal administrative moves resulted in the evaluation being completed by those who had not begun it. In general terms, the case studies confirm the basic principle of structuring the evaluation over a given period of time and of planning activities within that time frame. Probably, however, the concept of a formal workplan is not appropriate to the evaluation of social development. In the first instance, if the evaluation is being carried out 'in ideal circumstances', there would be less need for a purposefully mounted exercise after a given period of time when, for reasons of control and costs, a workplan might be appropriate. The essentially qualitative and multi-dimensional nature of the evaluation of social development makes it difficult to conceive of wrapping it all within a formal plan of activities.

(ii) The Selection of Indicators

In the case studies in Chapter 3 (and in particular the Zimbabwe and India cases) we can see the detail of how the indicators that were identified formed the basis for judgement in the evaluations of those two projects. More generally, however, we must conclude that the whole area of appropriate indicators for social development evaluation still needs further definition and experimentation. In one sense indicators are the key issue; without them any process of evaluation will lack a set of reference points for data collection and analysis. Essentially the problem encountered by the case studies was that, in most instances, the whole key area of objectives and appropriate indicators had not been dealt with satisfactorily before the project began; hence, for many it was an exercise of determining indicators only at the time of formal evaluation. The result of this was that, to a large extent, recourse was made to quantifiable indicators, as being less difficult to suggest and as guaranteeing a modicum of reliable data about project progress. There was little evidence in several of the case studies that the evaluators had come to terms in detail with the whole notion of what indicators should be used to evaluate a process of social development; essentially they had limited the exercise to a few readily manipulable quantitative indicators, an element of local involvement, well established survey method techniques and then the report.

The Zimbabwe Case Study further illustrates a second important aspect of the identification of indicators; the parallel identification of the criteria and phenomena which can be employed to give substance and form to the more qualitative indicators and thus make it possible to collect data and information. Without such criteria and phenomena, qualitative indicators are intangible and un-observable and often become limited to a few generalised comments. However, this is an area of social development evaluation which still needs a considerable amount of detailed study, particularly at the operational project level. The list of indicators in Box 4.4 from one of the Indian case studies illustrates the dilemma; how in fact do we use the notion of 'measurement' to those kinds of more intangible indicators listed, for example, under 'self-reliance' and 'social mobility'? Social development evaluation has certainly begun to recognise the crucial nature of these more qualitative indicators, but most such projects have yet to develop appropriate means of 'measuring' them.

Box 4.3
Identifying an Appropriate Indicator

An interesting example concerns a project of riverine fodder-crop (*panicum bourgou*) regeneration along the Niger river. It had been assumed by most people (particularly the technical services working in the area and external aid agencies) that the primary reason that groups were interested in this activity was in order to ensure adequate fodder for their animals during the dry season; and indeed a local people's indicator for measuring the success of the project was if they could offer visitors' calabashes of milk at a later date in the year than usual.

However discussions with women revealed a different criteria 'ask the children if they have drunk more *kundou* (a sweet drink also made from this fodder crop)'. Further discussion revealed this criterion for success was a single indicator that allowed rapid appraisal of several aspects of the project since if the *kundou* had been made available to the children it would indicate that there had been enough to satisfy the needs of the animals, given the men's control over production.

This process also indicated the different priorities given to the activity by men and women. This also indicates the importance of undertaking this kind of discussion on indicators before an activity starts so that a project might be modified or even not supported if it is revealed that it might have a deleterious effect on some groups.

Box 4.4
Indicators of Social Development

(a) Income Indicators
• increased income in cash or kind
• new sources of income
• greater stability and regularity of income
• reduced work requirement with regard to water, fodder and fuel

(b) Consumption Indicators
• changes in food consumption patterns; quality and regularity
• increased expenditure on education, health and non-food items
• improvements in living environment, e.g. dwelling, sanitation, etc
• asset creation, e.g. land, implements, animals
• acquisition of non-essential items/luxury goods

(c) Indicators of Self-Reliance
• greater independence in economic decision-making
• better knowledge of marketing opportunities
• higher level of household savings
• more use of public and private transport facilities
• reduced debt obligations to moneylenders
• less dependence on and increased bargaining power
vis-à-vis dominant social groups
• reduction in seasonal out-migration
• improved ability to cope with contingencies such as illness

(d) Indicators of Social Mobility
• greater willingness to approach public officials
• breaking-down of traditional caste barriers
• higher level of electoral participation
• increased participation in decision-making by women
• more mobility for women

(CASA, India)

The above set of indicators are probably representative of the current 'state of play' of the situation concerning indicators for social development evaluation and they probably go as far as we can for the moment. They represent a mixture of the more common-place, quantitative aspects of social development projects with areas of project activities—'self-reliance' and 'social mobility'—which are essentially qualitative in nature and which, correspondingly, are notoriously difficult to evaluate on the basis of time-specific, one-off evaluation. Furthermore the kinds of changes implicit in these suggested indicators, such as 'breaking down of traditional caste barriers', are not changes which we can attribute only to project activities. The task, however, is not insuperable; but the exercise is somewhat meticulous and time-consuming. It calls for the taking of a particular indicator, such as 'greater willingness to approach public officials', and its breaking down into the kinds of phenomena by which the indicator can be identified over time, the recording of this continuous identification, the collection and storing of the information, and its interpretation at a later stage in terms of 'progress' or 'changes' which have occurred. Regrettably the evidence to date suggests that few donor supported social development projects have yet to establish the internal mechanisms to allow them to undertake these tasks.

III. Reporting

The formal exercise of reporting, with its accompanying documents and notion of 'feed back', is a recognised but also an often neglected aspect of project evaluation. It is widely recognised as an intrinsic part of the process, but in practice it is often overwhelmed by both the sheer weight of documentation and the immediate demands of a donor agency. Whatever other 'principles of approach' may be stated beforehand, the writing-up of an evaluation is often dominated by the demands of the moment. In the evaluation of social development, two aspects of this writing-up tend to be emphasised:

(i) The importance of 'feed-back' from those more directly involved in the project. Feed-back is inevitably seen as critical in the sense that those who actually experience the project will have the opportunity to comment upon what the evaluators believe is resulting from the project's activities. In the Zimbabwe Case Study in Chapter 3, for example, we see in some detail the ways in which local feedback was built into the final preparation of the evaluation report. Generally in the case studies there was some process of consultation locally before a final report was prepared; yet it is difficult to conclude that this was done in any rigorous manner or that project participants, in most instances, had a realistic opportunity to debate and to finally agree the evaluator's report. The studies of Mali, Zimbabwe and Colombia were exceptions to this general trend; in the Ethiopian case study it was felt that project participants did not have the 'stamina' to contribute any direct feedback to the evaluation team's report.

(ii) The nature of the report which is eventually prepared on as part of the evaluation exercise. The three case studies in Chapter 3 illustrate this matter admirably and show the thought given to producing a report(s) which is both timely and intelligible. It could be argued that this indeed is the crucial stage of the whole evaluation exercise; if the report(s) is not shareable and not readably accessible to all involved, then the whole purpose of the exercise may have been defeated. The problem is summarised in Mark Robinson's case study for the Workshop:

> In another of the projects in the study, the preliminary field report was translated into the local language and circulated to all the grassroots organisations, which provided feedback via their representative who attended a meeting with the evaluation team. This was clearly the optimal way to proceed but it was not possible to do this in each of the four evaluations because of time constraints.

The above quote encapsulates the dilemma. By its nature, social development evaluation demands a continuous process of involvement by local people at all stages of the exercise; it is not something that can, where necessary, be dispensed with because of the demands of time or other obstacles. There are, therefore, still enormous strides to be made on the whole issue of evaluation reports. Lip-service inevitably is made to the importance of accessibility, consultation and genuine involvement; the pragmatic demands of donors and external evaluators often thwart such lofty principles.

IV. Reflection

Ideally social development evaluations (and indeed all evaluation exercises) should conclude with a period of 'reflection', during which the proceeding process can be examined with a view to arriving at a conclusion as to whether it was 'successful' or not. Having said that, however, it is not a question of measuring the 'success' of the process; it is more one of reflecting on the exercise and feeling confident, or not, about the outcome. Typically this 'reflection' is a structured exercise, often undertaken in the form of a workshop and takes place not immediately but fairly soon after the evaluation. The Case Studies in Chapter 3 above document this 'reflection' in some detail, particularly in the case of Zimbabwe, and serve to reinforce its importance. All of the Case Studies reported a period of 'reflection' after the evaluation, although the participants in this exercise varied considerably. In some cases the 'reflection' was limited to the evaluators and the more immediate agency staff; but several of the evaluations included a range of participants in this exercise, e.g. local people, institutions which had been involved in the evaluation, agency staff and evaluators. A sound principle might be to ensure that all the major actors who had contributed to the evaluation should participate in a post-evaluation 'reflection'; only in this way can they be informed of the progress and the outcome of their efforts.

More generally an examination of the various case studies reveals the following as four principal issues which arose during the period of 'reflection' at the end of the evaluation exercise:

(i) Many of the studies commented upon the general lack of preparation for the evaluation exercise. This comment referred essentially to two matters. First, the crucial importance of thinking through an exercise of the potential complexity of a social development evaluation, with all its nuances of 'process', 'participation', 'qualitative' and so on; it is a complex process and it needs careful thought and the 'time' factor becomes important. More than one study underlined the time issue in the sense that adequate time must be allowed for, not just in terms of a formal evaluation exercise at a particular moment in time but also during the evolution of the project in order to assess its progress. Second, and of equal importance, the need for adequate documentation as the information base for the evaluation. Most studies lamented the lack of an adequate information base, which perhaps reinforces the contention that social development evaluation must be an intrinsic and on-going part of the whole process and not merely an event at the end. Indeed it is inconceivable that any evaluation exercise can be undertaken if the project to be evaluated does not have a historical, appropriate and accessible information base. Again this whole issue becomes that much more complex when we talk of an 'information base' for the kinds of qualitative issues and changes with which a social development project might be dealing.

(ii) Although lip-service was made in most of the projects which were evaluated to the notion of 'participation', in several the evaluations undertaken were not as participatory as was hoped for. In many respects this was probably due to the fact that the projects themselves were not very participatory, a fact which would certainly influence any evaluation exercise. Other explanations referred to the time required and the difficulties involved in promoting this participation, to the inability of project beneficiaries to understand what the exercise was all about, to the defensiveness and apprehension of project staff and to the possible attitude of the evaluators which had not facilitated this participation. Box 4.5 provides an example from Ayele Gebre Mariam's case study of an evaluation in Ethiopia, which illustrates the kinds of behavioral and attitudinal problems which can arise with an externally led social development evaluation which, supposedly, will seek to involve local project staff and people. Whatever the explanation, several studies concluded that peoples' participation in the exercise had been lacking, which would seem to go against the very philosophy of social development. The studies were sanguine enough, however, to realise that this omission was not like forgetting a particular input into a project, which at a later date might be retrievable. It represented a major omission on the part of the project and one which would influence any evaluation exercise.

Box 4.5
Problems of Participation in
Social Development Evaluation

Some of the staff felt that the evaluation team was a fault finding mission, looking under stones and did not realise that evaluation is an educational intervention and is meant to empower the poor to initiate their own development. The project staff did not show cooperation with the team. They suspect that they may lose their positions if the outcome of the evaluation happens to be negative. The team members were seen as judges rather than facilitators, educators and collaborators, bringing together different processes and exercises in order to break down prejudices and assumptions.

Even though the evaluators tried to explain the purpose of the mission in different contexts, it was impossible to win the confidence of some of the senior project management staff.

(iii) Several studies concluded that, although they were satisfied with the general outcome of the evaluation, they had difficulties in managing non-quantifiable data and information. Such an observation is not unexpected since we still lack well proven examples of how this form of evaluation works. The Mali study reported that although the rural communities had been capable of analysing and assessing technical and economic activities, they had found it far more difficult to articulate their analysis of the 'social' outcomes of the project. In particular those evaluations which used an interview approach to data and information collection encountered problems both in handling structured and semi-structured interviews at the same time and also in aggregating the quantitative and qualitative data obtained. Clearly this issue continues to be a major difficulty in social development evaluation, but one which could be said to be caused by evaluators seeking to understand qualitative 'outcomes' with quantitative data collection techniques and not being ready to devise techniques more appropriate to this kind of outcome.

(iv) Techniques of self- or auto-evaluation are important and widely used in social development. Given the qualitative nature of this kind of development, auto-evaluation is perhaps the best way to get within the processes occurring and to give them some structure. Key qualitative outcomes of social development such as 'community organisation', 'solidarity', 'greater awareness' and so on can best be explained and structured by those directly experiencing the outcomes. Both project workers and participants must be given the chance also to reflect on their own roles and involvement in the process and be encouraged to verbalise how they see the outcome. Such an approach, however, is not without its problems:

> A self-evaluation demands a big amount of self-criticism on the part of the actors of an activity. The actor must be prepared to be very honest with himself in order to discover the problems and to be able to improve his work. This already is difficult. This self-criticism however is only possible if the actor knows that the results of the evaluation will not be used for sanctions and that he will be given a chance to improve failures discovered during the process of self-evaluation. If there is any real fear involved the actor will not be able to look at his work in a critical way and the self-evaluation will become a self justification. (GEAP, Mali)

Post-evaluation reflections also suggested that in social development evaluation the use of a team of external consultants is not enough; the team's work must be supplemented by the direct involvement of project beneficiaries and staff, not simply in terms of seeking their views but more importantly in involving them closely with the work of the team. The best way this can be achieved is by developing a permanent internal monitoring system which beneficiaries and staff would manage and which would be able to contribute to formal evaluations at a later stage. In projects where such systems do not exist, the whole exercise of social development evaluation becomes very much dependent upon the attitudes and skills available and upon the circumstances of the time.

Concluding Comments

The case studies would tend to confirm that, in comparison with say ten years ago, the concept of social development has become more widely understood and its evaluation has begun to be undertaken in an increasingly rigorous manner, which seeks not only to quantify results but also to explain project outcomes in a much broader and qualitative sense. However, and as the Colombia case study graphically illustrates, social development evaluation at the project level is still fraught with complications; it inevitably requires a concerted and dedicated effort to see the process through to completion. More positively, the beginnings of a framework (or set of operational references) to guide such evaluations is taking shape in different parts of the world and the evaluation exercise, which was for so long the monopoly of external agents, has undergone profound re-thinking. However, and despite the many examples brought out and issues raised in this chapter, there remain a number of aspects of social development evaluations which merit further enquiry:

(i) *Evaluation and Culture:* Underlying the whole process of evaluation as outlined in the case studies is the notion of 'culture' and the different perceptions that can exist of the process itself. Essentially it could be argued that evaluation should be context specific and that the whole paraphanelia of the evaluation exercise, with its repertoire of techniques and vocabulary, should be sensitive and adapted to local culture. One immediate aspect of this has been the undoubted increase in the past 10–15 years of the use of anthropologists in evaluation exercises. This issue of culture potentially has many facets; traditional politeness at receiving external visits, a reluctance to 'upset' an honoured guest, the inability to translate many terms associated with evaluation into local languages, the inappropriateness of direct questioning and a preference for more indirect and friendly enquiry, practices which influence the ability of women to participate in the exercise, reluctance to show excessive haste, and so on. Social development evaluation cannot be straight-jacketed into a set of universal practices; the tools it employs most be translated into the language, images and practice of the local culture. How often have we seen enumerators, questionnaire in hand, trailing after nomadic herdsmen and trying to complete ten interviews in a single day on the cost-effectiveness of camel dipping!

More concretely the issue of 'culture' is also played out in the interface between the external, Northern development agency and the Southern project holder. This playing out can manifest itself in different perceptions as to the rationale for the evaluation; an external imposition or an internal mechanism of project development. Both sides similarly may have different views concerning the usefulness or the role of the evaluation in the overall project process, on the appropriateness in the context of the evaluation procedures and methods to be employed and, for example, on what constitutes a 'benefit' from or an 'outcome' of the project. All of these issues serve to underline the central importance of recognising the potential existence of different perceptions of the various elements in an evaluation process. With more quantitative and tangible project objectives, different perceptions may be less evident; but in the evaluation of social development, with its emphasis upon qualitative change and local participation, different perceptions based on cultural differences may be more in evidence.

(ii) *Cost-effectiveness*: This is a potentially controversial issue but one which it is most appropriate to raise. With the emergence of the term 'process' in social development vocabulary and the implications of evaluation as an on-going process, as opposed to the more traditional one-off exercise, understandably the total costs involved in the whole exercise are beginning to be called into question. Similarly the cost-effectiveness of these processes of social development, which supposedly lead to an improvement in peoples' well-being, can also subjected to similar questioning. However, apart from Zimbabwe, the case studies offer little guidance on this issue, although it surfaced vigorously in discussion and was increasingly recognised as a relevant issue.

The evaluation of social development, in both a quantitative and a qualitative sense, gives the impression of being lengthy, labour intensive and a continual call on the resources of a project. In general terms we could ask, 'what are the costs of improving peoples' livelihoods via a process of social development, in comparison with other strategies which have the same objective?' In this we are not only referring to the actual financial costs of a project, but equally to the opportunity costs of staff spending so much time with the process. We can then ask the same set of questions about the evaluation of such social development projects. Further, a number of very debateable issues could be raised: 'do we always have to equate development in the first instance with some notion of financial cost?, 'is it always valid to put a cost on all time spent on a development activity in the sense of then judging whether it is justifiable?'; 'is there a standard unit cost for every increment of development to which all project should adhere?' It would appear that the debate about the cost-effectiveness of social development as a whole, and in particular of its evaluation, has now been joined and will gather in vigour in the coming years. The debate, of course, is not new and goes back to the continual debate on the relationship between, and the priority which should be given to the social as opposed to economic sectors in the overall development of a country. In the particular context of externally funded social development projects, however, it would appear that, particularly among the northern NGOs, this issue is being raised for the first time and substantially.

(iii) *The implications of peoples' participation:* If we add the ingredient of a participatory form of evaluation, then certain consequences arise which need to be analysed. In the first instance it must be said that many (social) development projects have little participatory basis; in these circumstances it is slightly absurd to talk of participatory evaluation. The existence of a visible and effective participatory basis to a project is a *sine qua non* for a participatory form of evaluation; if this basis does not exist, then it clearly is idle to talk of a participatory approach to the evaluation. Second, and as the Zimbabwe case study argues, a participatory approach implies time, patience and resources which a project must be prepared to commit; it is folly to believe that one can mount an authentically participatory form of evaluation if the above ingredients are in short supply. Third, there is often an over-exuberance concerning the usefulness of a participatory approach and projects can go overboard and see it is a kind of 'cure-all'; it is not and its use can be exaggerated. Participatory forms of evaluation often face the criticism of being 'unscientific' and lacking in intellectual rigour; such comments can be rebutted but only if the approach to the use of this form of evaluation is rigorous and is based upon a logical progression of activities.

(iv) *Information needs:* This refers to the importance of assessing what level of information would be necessary for effective social development evaluation. In one way this is a bit like asking the question, 'how long is a piece of string?'. But it is an important question since this form of evaluation seems to imply many people, over quite some time collecting possibly a considerable amount of information. There are no answers to this question. However, it surfaced consistently during discussions and clearly is a preoccupation for practitioners.

In terms of approaches to evaluating social development, the workshop confirmed that substantial and imaginative strides have been made in the past ten years or so. Development agencies are no longer solely dependent upon classical quantitative approaches to project evaluation, although it must be said that this classical paradigm is still dominant and many agencies, in their urgency to show results, often seek its safe haven. But 'alternative' approaches are now firmly on the agenda and the past decade has seen one major advance; the recognition of the need to understand both the quantitative and the qualitative outcomes of development projects. In this latter exercise there is little science and we continue to experiment with approaches and methods; but equally we are becoming more confident that the light at the end of the tunnel is getting closer.

CHAPTER FIVE

GUIDELINES FOR THE EVALUATION OF SOCIAL DEVELOPMENT PROGRAMMES

Introduction

The present guidelines are formed around the following five phases which characterise most evaluations: (I) Preparation, (II) Planning, (III) Execution, (IV) Reporting and Feedback; (V) Reflection and Action. In addition to these, we also raise the issues surrounding a preliminary stage of 'pre-planning', which should be considered even before the preparation of the evaluation.

One of the reasons for the addition of pre-planning to our schema was the strong feeling among many of our participants of the need to first take account of the context and conceptual framework in which the programme operated. Guidelines which tried to arrive at methods or 'tool kits' without due regard for these would be of limited value. Although there is a superficial attraction in providing straightforward techniques or tools which can be used in evaluation, in practice the ease of transfer of such tools has run into serious difficulties.

Pre-Planning

Conceptual framework

Underlying social development is always an implicit or explicit understanding that development is about social change or transformation. It is argued here that it is not possible to evaluate social development without being clear of the conceptual basis upon which the social development programme is built. An essential part of the pre-planning for the evaluation will be to identify as far as possible the conceptual, theoretical and even ideological foundations or origins from which the programme has emerged. It was argued strongly in the Workshop that such clarifications are necessary if we are to avoid the trap of using evaluation merely to maintain the status quo rather than reinforcing the movement of social development towards social transformation.

In the previous chapter we dwelt in detail on some aspects of the different approaches to social development. In the practice of evaluation, defining the conceptual framework may well be a brief exercise if it is explicitly stated in programme documents and commonly understood by most of those involved. If the conceptual framework of the programme is only held implicitly rather than made explicit, then further investigation may be needed to identify the conceptual framework. This will involve looking at written materials and holding discussions with programme staff, a process that may entail considerable time and frustration.

History

All development interventions have a history. Organisations often find their own histories uncomfortable and new staff, on their arrival, find it convenient to draw a new line from which to operate. Before embarking upon a major evaluation it is worth uncovering the historical context in which the programme was conceived and through which it operated. Many evaluations are guilty of evaluating against contemporary objectives and fashions rather than those which informed and underpinned the original intervention. The work required to identify the history of a programme often entails working through past files and can be carried out by research assistants in advance of beginning the evaluation itself. Basic material can be collated through this process which can be of use to those involved in the evaluation. It can provide basic financial information, early statements of objectives, previous evaluations or monitoring reports, lists of staff involved and so forth.

Context

A great deal of the context in which a programme works or has worked will emerge from its history. But it is important to spell out the changes in this context during the life of a programme. Important areas that need to be identified for the contextual background will include:

- *economic*–including major macro changes (e.g. food prices, inflation, government policies, exchange rates, etc), as well as micro or local changes (e.g. opening of a new road or market);

- *political*–including changes in government and changes in external relations (e.g. with dominant foreign partners);

- *organisational*–for example, a move away from a parent organisation, or development of a new structure;

- *social*–one of the key areas, and also most difficult, will be to identify the social context in which a programme operates (e.g. whether the work is with a particular ethnic minority). In some ways this social context may well be at the centre of a social development intervention. However, there will normally be important social and cultural characteristics which can be identified as pertinent, without having to mount a major research programme.

Defining purpose

Before going any further it must be asked if everyone agreed on what are the objectives of the programme? Is there a 'mission statement' as to the purpose of the programme? Later, it might well be necessary to undergo goal clarification exercises with different groups involved in the programme in order to see whether they know, share or understand its objectives. However, while goal clarification exercises can be a useful tool, at the pre-planning stage we are really interested in knowing whether those initiating an evaluation are clear about the programme goals before they proceed any further; and further, whether there are clear programme documents which detail the evolution of programme objectives over time.

Stage 1: Preparation

Negotiation

The first and one of the most important single parts of the preparatory process will be the negotiation of the objectives of an evaluation. At an early stage it will be necessary to:

(i) Be clear who is initiating the evaluation process and who has the power of decision making over both the evaluation and its outcomes.

(ii) Be clear who is being allowed access to the negotiation of the evaluation; who is being asked to comment, who is being excluded, and how far will varying opinions be taken into account?

(iii) Has time been allowed for this process of negotiation?

(iv) Is it possible for there to be more than one view of the purpose of the evaluation, and are these compatible or are they likely to conflict?

Many people feel that the two most important questions in any evaluation are: who has initiated the evaluation and who controls it (they need not be the same)? Once these are answered many of the stages and questions which follow may already be determined. Thus for example a decision by a foreign donor to initiate an evaluation for the purposes of accountability may well determine the whole shape and nature of subsequent evaluation. Equally a programme manager's decision to look at an evaluation from the point of view of staff performance will effect the whole way the evaluation evolves.

One useful exercise at this stage (and subsequent stages) is to carry out an analysis of stakeholders interested in the programme. This analysis should list all the individuals, or groups of people with an interest in the programme, along with their information requirements and their power in terms of decision making. Table 5.1 illustrates one way of doing this.

Table 5.1
Who is Involved in the Evaluation Process

Stakeholders	Their Interests	Information Required	Power in Decision Making

Another useful exercise is to clarify the different interests of different organisations involved in a typical social development evaluation. In the Workshop, a group produced a matrix which listed types of agency against some common purposes of evaluation. This is shown in Table 5.2.

The nature of the intended evaluation will have significant impact on the way in which the preparatory period is undertaken. If, for example, a participatory evaluation is expected, it will be important to ensure that those to be involved are also drawn into the preparation. Certain types of self evaluation may require specialised training in advance of the exercise itself.

Table 5.2
Purposes and Interests of Agencies
in Social Development Evaluation

Purpose of Evaluation	Type of Agency				
	CBO	Intermediary Southern NGO	Operational Northern NGO	Donor Northern NGO	Official Donor
Self-Interest					
Planning					
Problem Solving					
Accountability					
Justify Funding					
Education Training					

Decisions that may be taken lightly at this stage in the process may have long ranging implications. Many people feel that there is no need to worry too much about an evaluation until the evaluation has been set up and is under way. In reality certain decisions taken or not taken during the preparation will effect everything that happens thereafter. It will, for example, be difficult to mount a participatory evaluation if everything in the early stages is controlled totally by one person. A lack of consultation with key interested people at this stage will not be easy to compensate for later.

Stage 2: Planning

The Terms of Reference
It could be argued that the terms of reference (TOR) are the most important, single document in a social development evaluation exercise. It

brings together the different aspects of the negotiation, context, objectives and logistics of the evaluation. It will be more difficult to draw up the TOR if we are planning to enter into a process based evaluation where there is wide scope for participants to alter the way in which the evaluation develops. In general the TOR should allow for the unexpected, such as unforeseeable results, major new challenges or conflicts. However, even with a process-based, flexible evaluation it should be possible to fall back upon the TOR if they clearly set out the parameters within which the process operates. For example, one of the evaluations presented to the Workshop took place over a period of years and suffered through a number of key staff changes in the main agency. Clearly defined TOR for the evaluation process should ensure that changes in personnel do not easily destroy the long term dynamic of the evaluation.

This section brings together some of our experiences of TOR and provides a checklist to clarify any assumptions or premises upon which the TOR are based, and ensure that the TOR are sufficiently comprehensive for the task in hand.

Context of the TOR:

- are the TOR clear, and based on the objectives of the evaluation?

- is it clear what the composer of the TOR wants to know?

- who is controlling the evaluation process?

- are any other assumptions made by the commissioning agent entirely clear (e.g. philosophy, country strategy, 'mission statement' etc.)?

- is there scope for questioning or is this a 'managerial review' which accepts certain existing limitations (e.g. the project must continue regardless; senior management can do no wrong; the government cannot be questioned)?

- is this a donor driven review, a joint exercise, or partner driven etc.? Whichever it may be, be honest.

Writing the TOR:

- those who should be involved will depend in part on the objectives;

- imposed TOR will be more likely to cause tension;

• ideally, get the views of those effected or expected to 'participate' in the evaluation or provide them with the opportunity to contribute to it;

• the person who will have to take action on the TOR should have a chance to contribute to the TOR to ensure they produce what they want or expect.

Contents of the TOR:

• it should make clear the purpose behind the evaluation; the ownership of the process; and the use of the evaluation;

• place the evaluation in a context;

• set the objectives of the evaluation in relation to its purpose;

• operationalise the general objectives into specific questions and where possible prioritise them;

• define areas of special concern;

• make it clear how the team is to be composed, how it is to be structured (who is the leader and who has the last say in case of a disagreement);

• provide a outline person specification for the evaluation team in order to assist in deciding the sort of people required and their specific skills and qualifications;

• set a realistic time frame;

• agree the budget;

• outline the reporting requirements (length etc.);

• specify whether any follow up is required on behalf of the team (e.g. presentation of the report, revisiting the site later etc.).

Methodology

• is it important to specify in the TOR the methodology to be used?

• is the type of evaluation clear enough to indicate the appropriate methodology (e.g. a review of client satisfaction requires that they are asked for their views)?

• can the best method be afforded, or will compromise be necessary (either way do not expect a 'Rolls Royce' evaluation on a motorbike budget)?

• have the required qualitative and quantitative materials been defined?

The Evaluation Team

In choosing who is to be involved in any evaluation we are faced with two types of decision. Firstly, in drawing up the TOR we should already have specified the qualifications required of those in the evaluation team, as we should for any job description. This is relatively straightforward although frequently ignored. Thus if we require a Spanish speaking, female water engineer this is whom we should be hiring. Secondly, in addition to their professional suitability for the evaluation, the evaluators also need certain inter-personal qualities. In the Workshop several people mentioned that the character of the evaluator was crucial in the success or otherwise of their own experiences of evaluation. It is more difficult to proscribe guidelines on this; while we may all agree that having the right sort of 'sympathetic' person is important, we will never agree how that person could be defined and identified. A sympathetic person is not merely someone who agrees with us, but most importantly, someone who listens to all sides in an evaluation. The internal dynamics of a team should also be considered, to ensure a good mix of skills, experience and social characteristics (gender, ethnic group etc.).

Cost

There are different aspects of the cost of an evaluation which need to be considered:

(i) What can you afford? In an ideal world the answer to this question would be the same as that required to do the job in the best way possible. However, we are not in an ideal world, less so because we work for voluntary agencies and often have to work with limited resources. So we are obliged to make compromises and choose methods and approaches which might not be our first choice.

(ii) What costs could be justified by the size of the programme being evaluated? Obviously, very small programmes with budgets spreading over a few thousand pounds will not normally justify any major expenditure. Some agencies resolve this by either sampling; a representative number of small projects are chosen for in-depth evaluation. Other agencies only evaluate smaller projects for specific reasons (such as the experimental nature of the programme).

(iii) What is the opportunity cost to those involved in an evaluation? This question was raised several times during the Workshop in relationship to the more 'participatory' forms of evaluation. For example, it was noted that methods such as participatory rural appraisal could involve the poor in committing considerable amounts of time to participatory exercises (4 to 5 days might be normal). It was concluded that we should not discount too lightly the opportunity cost of the time of the people involved in evaluations, whether the staff of an agency, the poor, or other 'clients' of a programme. A careful assessment should be made as to whether the advantages of involving the people in the evaluation justifies absorbing large amounts of their time.

Although we would all like to be able to refer to basic guidelines on what an evaluation ought to cost, the Workshop was not able to come to any conclusion on this topic. Prices vary internationally, as do attitudes towards using expatriate evaluators (where ever they may come from), larger teams, professionals, and so forth, all of which will have a bearing on the total cost of an evaluation. Once the maximum financial limit for an evaluation has been identified the best we can do is to advise that common sense dictates actual expenditure. It should be clear that the size and scope of any evaluation should be weighed against its value to all the different interested groups or stakeholders.

Voluntary agencies often find problems in hiring good evaluators because the fees they are willing to offer are well below those available from other agencies. In part this comes from an ignorance of the prevailing market, and what the real gross costs of full time staff amount to. Thus many agencies are offering consultants rates well below what their full time staff are paid, if the real costs of full time staff are used rather than the basic salary (you can increase this by up to 40%). Voluntary agencies must face the reality of the changing market for consultants, who now find that due to changes in the funding structures of University and other institutions, are obliged to charge far more for their labour than previously.

A final note on the cost of evaluations which emerged from the Workshop was that despite their avowed interest in evaluations, donors seldom seem keen to pay for them. This has been especially the case when the evaluation has been requested by the agency implementing the programme, rather than by the funding organisation. Several Workshop members complained that donors were a limitation on their evaluation work. This seemed to go against the accepted wisdom that donors are the pressure behind evaluations which are 'imposed' on reluctant Southern partners. The reluctance seemed to be more on the part of Northern NGOS and other donors than Southern NGOS.

Timing
It is also important that an evaluation fits within certain parameters. For example, evaluations need to take account of the following:

(i) Availability of key actors.

(ii) Certain annual processes–for example, some programmes may only work in certain seasons (e.g. when migrant labourers swell an urban population).

(iii) Seasonal biases–many evaluations are carried out when it is easier to travel and visit, which may not be the best time to evaluate the impact of the programme. Alternatively it may be best to visit during the times when people are not fully absorbed in crucial work, such as harvesting, because they may be more able and willing to submit to interviews or participatory exercises.

(iv) The project or budget cycle. This is important from an organisational perspective, and therefore the TOR should specify a timetable to allow findings to be fed into certain key decision making processes or into the next planning or budgeting cycle.

Time
Many of the issues discussed above with regards to the cost of an evaluation will be pertinent to the amount of time it absorbs. In addition, participants in the Workshop stressed the need to ensure that the time required to participate in the evaluation was written into the routines of those to be involved. It will also be important when using external consultants that sufficient time is allowed for the whole process of recruiting evaluators. Too often agencies leave the recruitment process to the last minute and therefore find it difficult to obtain the services of appropriately experienced and qualified personnel. The amount of time otherwise required for any evaluation will also vary enormously depending upon the methodology used. In some circumstances it may be necessary to use very quick and dirty methods purely because time is not available for slower methods.

Base Line Data
During the Workshop it was frequently noted that one of the common

problems confronting NGOS is the lack of 'base line data' as the basis for mounting a social development programme evaluation. It is clear that if we follow a traditional approach to evaluation it is not strictly possible to evaluate in the absence of base line data. If we have no clear information as to the situation pertaining prior to an programme intervention then it becomes difficult both to evaluate the degree of any change and to assess the extent to which any change is due to the intervention rather than to other factors.

There seemed to be two common solutions to this problem. Firstly, many agencies build up their base line data through the life of the programme. Thus, good monitoring over time can provide the quality of information which can compensate for a lack of base line information. Some agencies use information on new groups joining a programme to provide comparison with those already involved in the programme. Secondly, some techniques now being used by NGOS, such as participatory rural appraisal and rapid rural appraisal, are being employed to collect base line data. As such these methods are relatively quick when compared to traditional survey techniques, although at such an early stage in the life of a programme they may create expectations and run into problems of acceptability with the client population. Experience has shown that PRA and similar methods have been successfully used to collect base line material, or as part of a needs assessment, where it has been carried out by an agency which already has a presence and identity in the area. Thus successful PRA's carried out by major agencies, such as the Aga Khan Foundation or Action Aid, have taken place where they already have several years of experience in the areas and the intention of continuing to work there.

Concluding Remarks on Preparation and Planning

A number of more general comments can be made about the pre-planning, preparation and planning stages of social development evaluation, including the following:

(i) Ensure the maximum degree of transparency, so that all those involved or who have an interest in the evaluation understand what is happening, why and when it is taking place, who is to be involved and how will it be conducted.

(ii) Clarity at all stages in key documents, such as the TOR, will help avoid confusion and misunderstandings. It is also hoped that by following our guidelines the final product of the evaluation will meet the expectations and requirements of those involved.

(iii) Despite the importance of planning, we all felt that flexibility should be maintained or even written in to the evaluation, to enable us to respond to the unexpected and to allow for new ideas and views from participants.

(iv) Anticipate conflict. Many evaluations flounder on the conflict between different interpretations of events and processes. There are ways in which this conflict can be absorbed by allowing different interest groups to articulate their views. Rather than wait until the conflict is open and the opinions are polarised, accommodate possible conflict in the planning of the evaluation, with space being allowed for dissenting views to be heard and recorded and groups to discuss and articulate their differences. In this way the evaluation team or person can assist as a facilitator.

(v) Make sure that a suitable evaluation team is selected. This definitely includes proper planning and timing as well as a good TOR and time to identify the right people for the job.

(vi) Be absolutely clear about what the objectives of the evaluation are and who it is hoped will benefit from the exercise.

(vii) Specify the underlying assumptions behind both the programme intervention and the evaluation; what is the philosophy of development which underpins them and the vision of social change which drives them?

Stage 3: Execution and the Choice of Methodologies

The choice of methodologies is perhaps the dominant issue surrounding the actual implementation of an evaluation. It is common practice in some areas for agencies to specify the methodology to be used in the TOR. Others, however reject this practice as they feel that there is a danger that inappropriate methodologies can be imposed by the commissioning agency, or the same favoured methodology becomes used regardless of the purpose and nature of the evaluation. Indeed it would seem more logical to go through some of the steps noted in our sections on 'preparation', and production of the TOR before making any commitment to a specific method.

Certain basic questions should be answered before choosing a methodology for the evaluation. For example, it could be argued one of the first issues to resolve is the decision whether the evaluation would be an entirely internal affair, using staff or clients of the programme, or an external affair, using evaluators from outside the agency. Secondly it has to be agreed whether a longitudinal evaluation spread over time was required or a short snap shot of the programme.

One approach to choosing a methodology is to try to make the decision as to which method would best provide the information required by a pre-determined selection of indicators. Our argument is, however, that it can be very dangerous to pre-select all the indicators likely to be important to the participants in a process of social development. It is important to first recognise the differences of perception and expectations of those involved before making any decision as to what indicators should be used. Using pre-selected indicators will lead to the wrong questions being asked, and more fundamentally, reflects a misunderstanding of what social development is about.

It would be convenient if it were possible to make an exact match between certain evaluation needs and specific methodologies. At the Workshop several approaches were tried which, it was hoped, would provide an agreed correlation between methods and needs. A great deal of time was spent first trying to establish the advantages and disadvantages of different methods, and secondly matching the common evaluation objectives against available methods. Subsequently we have worked with several other groups, primarily from NGOs to review evaluation purposes, characteristics and methods. Table 5.3 reproduces a compilation of experience and shows how common methods for generating information can first be assessed crudely in terms of their cost, the time they involve, expertise required and accuracy. These characteristics are supported by some general comments.

We have made an important, and often neglected distinction between those methods used for generating information and those for analysing it. Thus column 4 lists methods for analysing information against the methods used to collect this information. Finally, column 5 provides some hints as to which purposes the preceding methods could usefully contribute.

Methods for Generating Information

Participatory techniques
In general, a high level of participation should reduce the costs of an evaluation and the need for highly skilled outsiders. However, some of the recent development have created their own new professionals. Thus many of the techniques used within PRA (wealth ranking, mapping, venn diagrams) require facilitators to be trained before they can be used in the field. Furthermore, guided self evaluation usually requires some degree of external presence to act as a facilitator to the process. Such techniques do

INFORMATION GENERATION	METHOD OF ANALYSIS				CHARACTERISTICS OF INFORMATION
	COST	TIME	EXPERTISE	ACCURACY	COMMENT, GOOD FOR...
PARTICIPATORY TECHNIQUES	*	***	**	**	Views of beneficiaries, but high opportunity cost. Part of the development process itself.
FOCUS GROUP DISCUSSIONS	*	***	***	*	Potential problems organising groups but good direct flow of information.
FORMAL SOCIAL SURVEYS	***	**	***	***	Quantitative, how many and what type of questions.
INTERVIEWS	**	**	***	**	Both quantative and qualitative Information Possible. Depends on quality of interviewers/information
FORMAL REPORTING SYSTEMS	*	*	**	**	Depends on quality of monitoring. Good for background information.
OBSERVATIONS	*	**	***	***	Only as good as person making the observations
PARTICIPANT OBSERVATION	*	***	**	**	Good – sometimes essential – for understanding of target group and impact
SECONDARY INFORMATION	*	*	*	N / A	Complementary. Saves unnecessary info. Good for comparison.
GEOGRAPHICAL SYSTEMS	***	*	***	***	Good for physical data. Assumes relevance.
TECHNICAL SURVEYS	*	*	***	***	Save as above
FINANCIAL / AUDIT	**	**	***	***	Good for financial assessment. Less so impact, social relations.

METHOD OF ANALYSIS	PURPOSE OF ANALYSIS
	Accountability Up / Down, Planning, Control, Information (Info), Development Process, Impact, Profitability
Logical **F**ramework **A**nalysis, **P**articipatory **A**nalysis	Accountability Down, Info, Development Process, Impact (unintended), Planning. **Not** Control and Profitability.
Informed **O**pinion	Development Process, Info, Planning. **Not** Control?, Profitability?, Accountability?
Social **C**ost-**B**enefit Analysis, **S**tatistical **A**nalysis, **LFA, PA**	Accountability Up, (sometimes Development Process), Planning, Control, Info, (sometimes Impact).
SA, LFA	Info, Accountability Up, Planning, Control. **Not** Accountability Down, Development Process, Profitability.
LFA, PA, SA	Accountability Up, Profitability, (Impact?), Control, Planning. **Not** Development Process, Qualitative Impact.
IO	Impact, Info, Accountability Up, **Not** Development Process, Profitability, Control, Accountability Down.
IO	Info, Planning Indirect. Very Good for Impact. **Not** Development Process, Control, Profitability, Accountability Up/Down.
IO	Info, Planning. **Not** Development Process, Impact, etc.
IO, SA, SCBA	Info, Planning, Profitability, Accountability Up, Impact. **Not** Accountability Down, Control, Development Process.
IO, SA, SCBA	As Above
SA, SCBA	Accountability, Control, Planning. **Not** Impact, Development

however ensure that the views of clients, junior field workers and others are fed into the process of evaluation. Indeed the very act of participating in an evaluation can itself be empowering for the participants. Ironically, participatory techniques can also provide information which can easily then be fed into more formal methods of analysis such as logical framework analysis (or ZOPP). Participatory techniques are probably not the best if we are looking for a method which will increase the level of managerial control or financial accountability.

It should be added that there are many different techniques which are participatory, some of which have gained recognition, others of which have been used for many years without having attracted a name or following. What they share in common is their openness to ensure the maximum transparency and participation by the stakeholders and interested parties to a programme being evaluated (see, for example, Pratt and Loizos 1992, and Feuerstein 1986).

Focus Group Discussions

Focus group discussions are very commonly used by NGOs partly because they are relatively inexpensive and do not require a high degree of technical expertise. They also permit the evaluator to talk directly to the different stakeholders. Groups can be brought together which share similar social characteristics (e.g. all junior staff, or a collection of street children, women in a neighbourhood committee). Or a group can bring together a mix of people (representatives of different groups of staff, members of different community committees, men and women from a cooperative etc). Where representatives of different groups are brought together this can assist the process of dialogue and negotiation between different stakeholders' perceptions.

Focus group discussions have a further advantage in that they can allow views to gain some degree of collective approval. In some focus group discussions, ranking methods are used to illustrate the degree of consensus within the group over a certain issue of opinion. For example, in groups involved in an exercise to demonstrate the perceptions of poverty held by villagers in an African country, the facilitators encouraged groups to rank the degree to which they all agreed to certain statements made in the discussions. Individuals can also venture opinions in a group which they can state as collective wisdom and in doing so disassociate themselves from the act or opinion. For example, they may state that many people beat their children as a form of punishment. If they did this in a face to face interview they might fear that this would be interpreted as a confession that they are involved in such a practice.

Formal social surveys

Although social surveys may be costly and require time and external skills, they may still be one of the most accurate forms of collecting information. The question remains do we need such great accuracy, and do we need the quantity of data provided by a survey? Occasionally the answer will be yes, in which case the survey is a tried and test way of obtaining information which can feed into quantitative forms of analysis (see, for example, Nichols 1991, and Casley and Lury 1981).

Surveys are good at answering questions of 'how many?'. They can be used to assess the impact of a programme where it is possible to produce simple questions or other measurable indicators (numbers immunised, numbers using a water well, etc). Such surveys are less useful where it is not possible to use closed questionnaires and other straightforward measuring techniques. A great deal of social development does not lend itself to the sort of quantitative indicators appropriate to formal survey work.

Interviews

There are two types of interview, structured and unstructured. Structured interviews rely on a predetermined set of questions being asked in an interview in a set order. There is little room for digression and therefore questions must be relatively simple to avoid the possibility of answers being too long or moving away from the original question. Most of the points made about formal surveys will be relevant when considering structured interviews. It may be possible, however, to consider questions within an interview which measure attitudes if the person giving the interview is well trained and the questions carefully designed.

An unstructured interview permits questions to be more flexible. It allows the person interviewing to follow interesting and unpredicted lines of investigation. It also allows people to put things into their own words rather than be constrained by a series of previously agreed answers. In the hands of good interviewers, the unstructured interview can elicit qualitative information, although by the nature of the interview it may not be possible to compare the answers in a qualitative manner.

Occasionally it will be possible to design an interview which combines the advantage of both structured and unstructured questions into a single interview. In this case it will be advisable to ensure that interviewers are clearly instructed as to when they need to stick to the closed structure of the interview and when they are allowed to expand upon the initial question.

Many interviews rely heavily upon what are commonly known as 'key informants'. This usually entails detailed questioning of one or two individuals. Ideally such people should have an overview of the programme or area. However, they often tend to be professional informants, who are used regularly by all visiting interviewers. They also tend frequently to be people on the edge of a community, such as a school teacher, or someone who has married into a village. Their answers may be full of insight but are not entirely representative of the community. For the purposes of evaluation, key informants should be treated with caution as they may have their own biases and opinions which colour their replies.

Formal Reporting and Monitoring Systems

Depending on the quality of monitoring systems being used, a great deal of pertinent information should be generated as a part of the normal working of a programme. Internal monitoring should allow the maximum scope for stakeholders to feed in their views and opinions as to the progress of not of the programme. Participatory monitoring techniques such as those described in the case study from Colombia of Promesa are more likely to be appropriate to programmes with a genuine commitment to social development.

Legal and donor requirements will necessitate that certain traditional financial and narrative reports are produced. These may have a value for the purposes of evaluation and should not be assembled in such a way that they weaken rather than support the process of social development. Basic information will be important even for the most experimental and process-based programmes. There is no support on our part for the view that there is a complete contradiction between process-based social development on the one hand and normal good practice in reporting and accounting on the other.

Observation

In practice, most NGOs still rely heavily upon the reported observations of an individual for a large proportion of their evaluative material. There are some good reasons for this, such as the expense of alternatives and limited resources at the disposal of many NGOs. However, there are also certain, less satisfactory, justifications for the reliance on observation or informed opinion in evaluations. These have to do with agencies hiring people who will not ask critical questions but rather are trusted to reflect the values and opinions of the commissioning agency. Nonetheless, the observations of experienced 'evaluators' will inevitably play a part in most evaluation methods. Where we have some concerns is where such opinion becomes the only source of information and analysis.

Participant Observation

There is an increasing interest in the use of 'anthropological' methods of data collection given the long tradition in anthropology of studying social processes in sometimes difficult circumstances. Participant observation is a well tried method and its advantages and disadvantages are well known. From our perspective it holds one very strong strength in that it permits us to record and monitor the changes in a society from close quarters over a longer period than virtually any other method. It should be seen as a valuable complement to other methods.

Technical methods

Although we have noted technical methods in Table 5.3, these are less likely to be useful in evaluating social development than they might be for more direct service or technical interventions. Technical surveys of health coverage, or Geographical Information Systems (GIS) used to review livestock numbers or tree cover, will only be of secondary interest for the evaluation of social development as we have defined it. It is conceivable that they could be useful in reviewing specific outcomes of certain forms of intervention or the activities of community organisations.

Methods for analysing information

Some of the methods used for collecting information will also lead naturally into certain forms of analysis. However as noted previously it is important to make a distinction between these two stages. What also becomes clear is that there does seem to be a more limited numbers of methods for analysing and assembling information than can be called upon for collecting such material. It is interesting to note that we seem to be dependent upon either the statistical forms (cost benefit analysis etc), or logical framework analysis, or variations on an 'informed opinion', which usually means the opinion of the person or group designated as report writers. This apparent lack of alternatives should demonstrate to us the importance of ensuring that we allow sufficient time, and resources to carry out a thorough analysis of the information at our disposal.

The following section will review in some detail the way in which evaluation findings are presented and used. To conclude the present section on executing the evaluation, we should recall that it is important to bring together as much as possible in a single text the perspectives of the different stakeholders. This text should be shared with these stakeholders, ideally prior to a final draft being completed.

Measuring the Process: How Evaluations are Used

Introduction

Evidence suggests that often evaluations carried out by NGOs remained shelved documents and their results are not used as feedback for the further development of the programme. In reviewing the experience of NGOs in evaluation this harsh truth is repeated consistently. Considerable resources may be expended on evaluations so it seems strange that they are not used to the maximum possible extent. In light of the growing interest by NGOs in evaluation and in particular of social development programmes, why do so many of our agencies fail to fully utilise the product of evaluations?

In the Workshop two major factors relating to the use of evaluation material were considered. Firstly, the more conventional response is that NGO management structures and managers, fail to listen, absorb and act upon evaluation findings. Secondly, insufficient NGO staff are convinced by or understand the way in which the evaluation can itself be an integral part of the process of social development.

There are however certain common problems which have a negative impact on both of these facets of evaluating social development. One is the crucial relationship between the way information is used and the purposes for which it was obtained. In an earlier section of this book we dwelt upon the importance of clarifying the purposes and objectives of an evaluation. The key questions relating to this will have a very direct bearing upon the later uses of the evaluation.

In the image described in the Prajwala Case Study in Chapter 3, the development agency is regarded as a tree. This model simplifies the major aspects of a programme to be evaluated:

- the ideology (assumptions): *the ground*

- infrastructure (resources, management): *the trunk*

- activities: *the branches*

- impact: *the fruit*

Prajwala argued that it is possible to obtain the perspectives from all parts of the tree of what they think about the tree as a whole. This is achieved through sensitive evaluation which uses different methods to review the different component parts of the tree.

Another schema elaborates on this by taking the traditional line management hierarchy and argues for different evaluations or at least different methodologies for the different levels (see Figure 5.1). The role of the evaluator is to facilitate reviews of the different levels and to bring them together. Additionally the evaluator coordinates the process of negotiation and discussion between the actors or stakeholders from the different levels in the management structure.

Figure 5.1
Organisational Approaches to Evaluation

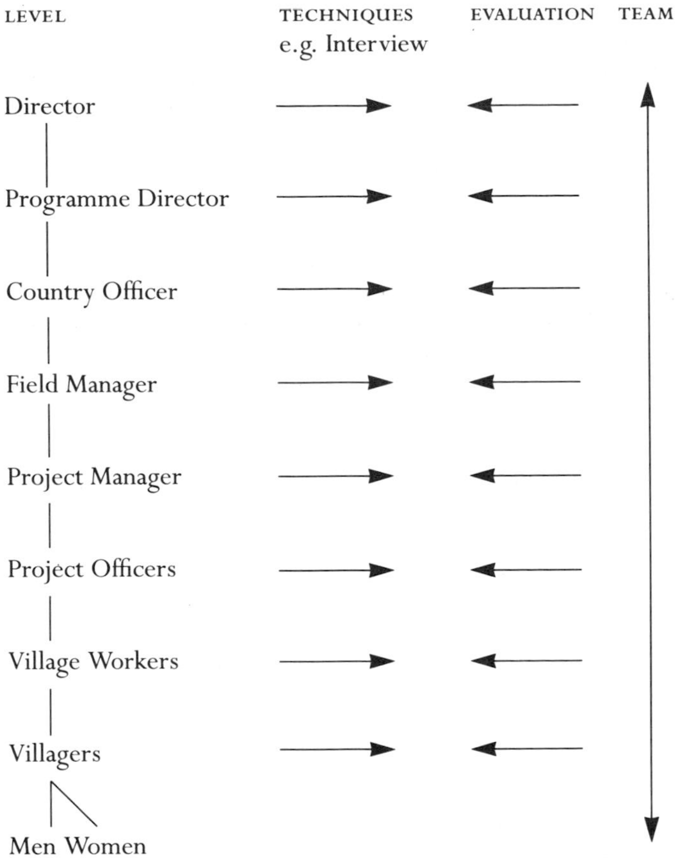

LEVEL	TECHNIQUES e.g. Interview	EVALUATION	TEAM

Director

Programme Director

Country Officer

Field Manager

Project Manager

Project Officers

Village Workers

Villagers

Men Women

In our review of NGO evaluations and of the experiences encountered in their inadequate use, the importance of certain values became clear, including:

Clarity: why is the evaluation being carried out etc?

Transparency: who is this for, what do they want from it?

Honesty: if an audit is required then do an audit not an evaluation of social processes and vice versa.

There is a very strong feeling that many development agencies have been guilty of using evaluations for the wrong reasons. Examples have been provided of agencies commonly using evaluations to fill in gaps in basic information and thus reducing the evaluation to an exercise in collecting base line data. In other agencies, audits have been disguised as evaluations of social processes and many hidden agendas have lurked beneath evaluations. In Table 5.4 we reproduce, with minimal editing, a chart listing the way evaluations can be used by different groups. It is interesting to note how many of these are either explicitly negative or indirectly have a negative developmental impact. The conclusion is that there must be a very clear statement of purpose and the appropriate method to meet it; or in the words of one Workshop participant, 'do not use a kitchen knife for gardening.'

Table 5.4
Uses of Evaluation–some possible reactions by different actors

FUNDERS
- Fundraising
- Personal research
- Justify existence
- Planning/design
- Decision making
- Allocation of resources
- Information gathering
- Prioritisation
- Replication and information sharing
- Influence programme
- Introduce new ways of work
- Dialogue
- Habit

LOCAL NGO
- Accountability
- Justify existence
- Performance assessment
- Course correction
- Planning/design
- Fundraising
- Political defence
- Impact assessment
- Networking
- Staff management
- Policy renew
- Structural reorganisation
- Needs assessment
- Situation analysis
- Review the mission
- Resolve conflict
- Clarify expectations
- Advice and training
- Planning and monitoring
- Educational tool
- Exaggerate achievements
- Expansion
- Personal research

BENEFICARIES/CLIENTS
- Exposes NGOS
- Improve services they receive
- Opportunities for expressing feelings
- Dialogue and dissatisfaction
- Test assumptions
- Independence
- Question leadership
- Take initiatives
- Control NGOS
- To find out what is being done in their name
- To voice expectations

The mechanical aspects of defining the evaluation purpose are also important if the material is to be used as intended. Thus a well constructed terms of reference should specify how the evaluation is to be handled once the data collection has been completed and the 'report' is ready for discussion and diffusion. It should be clear:

- who is to receive the report;

- who will be expected to act upon it;

- what format the material will be presented in;

- whether different versions are to be prepared etc.

Some of these questions will be reviewed in greater detail below.

Although the present Guidelines argue for the maximum degree of transparency in evaluations this is not the same thing as flooding everyone with irrelevant or confidential information. In any evaluation there will be material which should perhaps not be circulated widely (for example on the personal problems of individuals on the staff, or an aspect of the programme which might cause security risks for individuals). Indeed there is a strong argument for producing different versions or edited notes for different readers. Some evaluators have argued strongly for the concept of 'optimal ignorance' referring to the amount of information actually required for the needs of the reader. This they favourably compare to the alternative of 'data fetishism' where an addiction to the quantity of data overcomes both common sense and the needs of the people involved in the evaluation.

Sensitivity and honesty are required if a major evaluation exercise is to be reported differently to the range of stakeholder groups. There is a danger that the selection process can reinforce the many negative tendencies already at play, such as 'managerialism' even in the best evaluation (see below for further discussion on the issue of managerialism).

There is an unfortunate tendency for many agencies to regard evaluation as a necessary or imposed evil to be endured. In such cases we should not be surprised to find that little attention is paid to how the results of evaluation exercises are to be used. If the act of commissioning an evaluation or 'participating in it' is considered to be the minimum required to satisfy donors, boards or contemporary fashion then the 'report' becomes an irrelevance. In such a scenario then it is only to be expected that agencies do not learn and that staff and project beneficiaries in turn feel the imposition of such ill conceived exercises. If the time of staff and communities has been demanded for interviews, surveys and meetings without providing them the common courtesy of some feedback, then another generation of people will internalise a negative feeling about evaluation.

In the schema reproduced from the Workshop as Figure 5.2, we have repeated the simple progression from purpose, through method, to use in the undertaking of a social development evaluation. The elements of use we considered were feedback, the report, action on recommendations and follow-up. All of these were considered both in terms of the basic issues underlying any attempt to use evaluations and in terms of the confines on use which result from the general orientations held by different agencies.

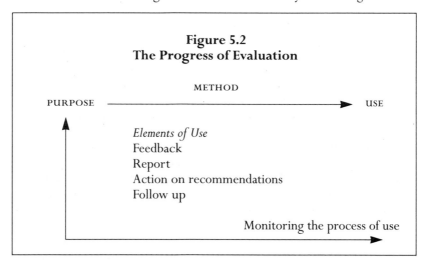

Figure 5.2
The Progress of Evaluation

METHOD

PURPOSE ⟶ USE

Elements of Use
Feedback
Report
Action on recommendations
Follow up

Monitoring the process of use

Management and Managerialism

In the project cycle followed by most NGOs the follow-up of evaluations should ideally lead to:

• institutional learning;

• amendment to existing and future project activities;

• improvement in project design;

• improvement in the impact and efficiency of the programme on behalf of the clients or beneficiaries.

Figure 5.3 describes a typical project cycle; from an 'idea' there is a progression through design, appraisal, implementation, and eventually onto monitoring and evaluation. Where the cycle goes wrong is that after evaluation instead of the information informing future projects through the next cycle the evaluation is lost to the public domain and leads nowhere. Hence the arrow which breaks away from the circle and disappears into the outer darkness of the forgotten filing cabinet.

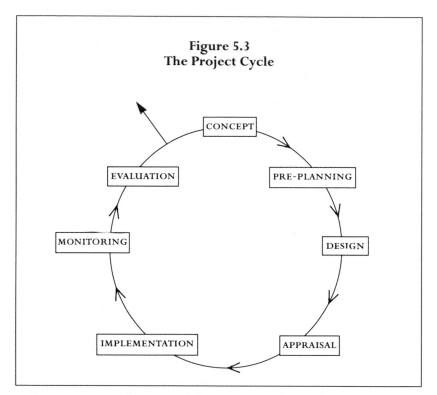

Figure 5.3
The Project Cycle

It is management's responsibility to ensure that evaluations are acted upon and fed into an organisation. Assuming that the interest in evaluation is genuine, the failure to properly follow-up evaluation findings are a sign of poor management. As noted above, the first step in following up an evaluation should come at the beginning of the process when the evaluation is first being commissioned. The purpose of the exercise should be clear to all participants. There should not be too many overlapping or even contradictory objectives. All this must be clearly presented in a terms of reference which has been negotiated by the different actors with an interest in the evaluation.

The second step should be to write into the TOR how the evaluation will be followed up, and in what form and to whom the findings will be disseminated. It is important to foresee any management implications of the evaluation and consequent decisions and to specify, if appropriate, who is expected to take action on these. Furthermore it should be clear who is responsible for ensuring that recommendations and decisions are reviewed in light of the evaluation.

Besides specifying areas of responsibility it is also worth considering details such as the timing of the presentation of reports. For example it is distressingly common for evaluation reports to arrive after crucial decisions have already been made regarding the project. If further phases of the project are to be implemented, then any design work should be informed by the evaluation. Sufficient time also needs to be allowed after the evaluation to permit the views of other actors such as staff, and partners to be articulated prior to making decisions. As a general rule however, it is recommended that evaluations are not tied to funding decisions but these are not the only management decisions for which the evaluation can be used. This point is illustrated in the example provided in Box 5.1.

Box 5.1

The project had already been ordered to close by a head office on the basis that it had fulfilled its task of providing emergency assistance to refugees. The evaluation team arrived as the engineers and others were already packing to leave. The evaluation showed that the engineers were providing a very needed service to local non-refugee communities, unbeknown to the head office. However it was too late for the findings of the evaluation team to reverse the order to close down the programme.

Accountability is a frequently used word in relation to evaluations. It is the case, however, that almost invariably the accountability works only one way in most NGOs, that being upwards to donors and senior management. It is still unusual for development agencies, whether Northern or Southern based, to feel obliged to be accountable downwards to their clients, partners or beneficiaries. Part of a good agency's responsibility should be to ensure that its work is accountable both ways. This will effect various aspects of the evaluation design, not least in the way any report is disseminated and discussed. As noted below, the method of dissemination should be appropriate to the clientele. This may require shorter written reports for certain readers or visual presentations for non-literate groups.

One common risk in all evaluation is what Guba and Lincoln have called 'managerialism' (Guba and Lincoln 1989:32). Managerialism refers to the rather too cosy relationship between the managers who commission evaluations and the evaluator. There is, they argue a tendency for managers to pre-determine the outcome of the evaluation through their relationship with the evaluator. They may choose an evaluator known to agree already with their views, or may write the TOR in such a way as to bias the data collection and analysis. And at the end of the process they can ensure, through contractual obligations, that the evaluation report can be buried if it is in any way uncomfortable for them. Thus, while many evaluations purport to have an open remit, they often have certain areas which are excluded from review and open discussion.

Another study of consultancy methods in the commercial field describes the traditional model as the 'mafia' approach. By this they are referring to the tradition of consultants or evaluators being hired by senior, and often new, managers to provide the justification for a previously determined course of radical action. This leads to major changes in staffing, redundancies, re-structuring, re-organisation, closure of departments and projects. The dramatic way it is carried out leads to the 'mafia' label which conjures up images of 'hit squads, hatchet men,' and the like (see Stebbins and Abrahams 1989).

In the managerial approach, the aspects of the work relating to the senior management team that commissioned the evaluation are deliberately excluded from the evaluation. Managerialism does little for two way accountability and often hinders organisational learning. Furthermore it deliberately chooses not to recognise that all the different actors involved in a programme and effected by an evaluation have their own perspectives, and rights as well as obligations.

It is clear to most people that a key element in evaluation is to identify the locus of power at an early stage. In the world of NGO development, power traditionally lies with the donors, and within donor agencies, with those making funding decisions. There is not a great deal of democratic decision making over the allocation of resources within most donor agencies and partners are rarely consulted by donors.

Traditional management thinking has stressed that evaluations are a tool to decision making at the disposal of senior managers. However, if we are to see the evaluation of social development as a part of the process of social development then it is not good enough to simply accept these precepts. A strictly hierarchical approach to the role of evaluation is to deny many of the underlying aims of social development and to conserve a top down approach to development.

Matching Means, Methods and Uses

There is a critical need to ensure an appropriate match between the design of the evaluation and its purposes and uses. Certain methodologies were perceived to be more likely to suit certain uses. Thus, for example, some methods produce better quantifiable data (social surveys, structured interviews, physical measurement), whilst others ensure a good representation of views from those involved in the project (group meetings, informal interviews, participatory techniques). It is essential that the choice of method is appropriate to the uses to which the evaluation is to be directed (Pratt and Loizos 1993).

There are many examples of evaluations where there has not been a satisfactory matching of means and uses, with consequent conflict and dissatisfaction. In other evaluations a great deal of unnecessary information is collected bearing little relevance to the needs and objectives of the evaluation. A recent review by one agency of its evaluations showed how few evaluators had systematically asked people what they actually thought of the programme being evaluated. There was a clear incongruence between the objectives of participatory projects and evaluations which were clearly non-participatory!

The Multi-layered Approach

Successful evaluations of social development activities will recognise that the different actors being evaluated will often have very different perspectives, opinions and experiences. Even the same events, or relationships will be viewed very differently by those involved. It is this apparent truism which has vexed so many people in search of a single objective reality. A great deal of academic literature has focused on the clash between the scientific rationalists and the relativists; the former believe in the single, observable, objectively verifiable reality, and the latter regard the world as being composed of a multitude of different realities, sometimes overlapping or even contradicting one another.

In terms of our concern over how to use evaluations of social development, we argue for an approach which accepts that those involved in an evaluation will have different perspectives which should all be recognised as having a validity in their own terms. For example, a small NGO dedicated to providing support to women's groups could be considered simultaneously from the following perspectives:

- as being defenders of the rural poor, by a middle class supporter;

- as providers of welfare, by a donor;

- as undermining local religions, by a local priest or imam;

- as undermining the family, by the husbands;

- as strengthening family values, by the field worker;

- as undermining the State, by the government officer;

- as weakening the political party, by the party officer;
- as fighting for women's rights, by the project director.

The list is endless, and hopefully familiar. An evaluation must recognise these different perspectives and must not ignore them or force them into an artificial consensus.

A good evaluation process will place all the different perspectives before those involved and facilitate an exchange between the different actors. This process of what some call 'negotiation' (Guba and Lincoln 1989) should make the evaluation a dynamic process. It should permit the different actors to respond to the perspectives of others. For example, the field workers should be allowed to justify why they feel the husbands are misguided and why the women's groups stand to strengthen not undermine the family; or permit the project director to argue why her work is not undermining the State and local parties but assisting women to operate as political equals.

This approach allows each group to make their own choice of indicators rather than regarding indicators as a series of totally objective sets of information. The approach recommended here recognises that different indicators will be relevant to different actors. Indeed the indicators chosen will reflect different perceptions of the development process and how these differing perceptions relate to the different contexts in which people live.

The negotiation process should not be interpreted too literally; the idea is that the process of evaluation should provide opportunities for the different perspectives to emerge and be discussed. The negotiation does not necessarily require face to face debate between the actors, but may entail a facilitated process of discussion through the evaluators. Again, if a formal written report is produced which highlights the different perspectives found by the evaluation team, then this can facilitate the negotiation process. The range of actors reading or being presented with the report will then have the opportunity to appreciate, comment, disagree, reflect and act upon these differences. The use of a 'stakeholder analysis' as described earlier will greatly facilitate this process.

The way in which an evaluation is used can be as productive and dynamic as the process of social development itself. If we accept that social development is concerned with, amongst other things, empowering people through improving their access to information, then evaluation can contribute towards this process. The process of evaluation can assist people to identify different sources of power, interests and areas of conflict. A participatory and open evaluation can bring new sources of information and insights to people previously unable to obtain access to such information. The discussions and 'negotiations' over aspects of the evaluation can bring clients closer to the point of controlling the programme and their own destinies.

The evaluation report should be the beginning of a new stage in the process, not the finale. It should open the doors to a phase of reflection facilitated by the insights it provides, in turn leading to further actions. Such a process will not occur unless actively designed into the evaluation with concrete steps taken for the dissemination and discussion of the evaluation findings.

In some cases, printing and distributing copies of the report may be sufficient where all those concerned are literate and able to articulate their responses to a formal report. Where people are not accustomed to dealing with dense written reports it will be necessary to produce the finding in other forms. Where literacy levels are minimal a very short summary in simple language may help. Alternatively personal verbal presentations using clear visual aids can feed back information to non-literate groups of staff or programme beneficiaries. There are some fine examples where theatre and other forms have been utilised to explain to poor communities the results of surveys encompassing them (see R. Trivedy, Appendix 6 in Pratt and Loizos 1993).

One way to ensure that the reactions to the evaluation from different people are recorded is to ensure that members of the evaluation team are involved in the follow-up. Through using the evaluation as a point for reflection, the evaluators can capture different reactions and facilitate inter-group discussion and negotiation.

Where external evaluators are involved they should present initial findings to people in the agency under scrutiny before they leave the project area. This allows for any misunderstandings and errors of fact to be clarified and allows those being 'evaluated' to respond and consider the draft recommendations. Where this works well it enables those directly involved to start the process of reflection and to take actions they consider important long before the formal and final report starts to make its way back to them. For example, in a case study from Zimbabwe by Redd Barna action took place as a result of an evaluation well before the final report was received.

Common practice at the moment seems to be to dispense with the evaluator once the formal report is written and presented to the commissioning agent. It would seem that most evaluators depart from the stage at the precise point at which their skills and role as a facilitator are most required. In saying this we are assuming that the evaluator has not fallen into the trap of 'managerialism' or the 'mafia model' and produced a report merely confirming a path of action desired by senior management. If they have done this then perhaps it is best that they do leave the scene quickly before the fighting begins! In evaluations using a more open or process approach it is often useful to bring the evaluators back after a short time (months rather than years) to review the way in which the evaluation has progressed through the organisation. At such times they can facilitate a has progressed through the organisation. At such times they can facilitate a new round of negotiation over key elements in the report and ensure that areas of confusion or disagreement are adequately aired.

Institutional Learning

Evaluation should play a crucial role in the longer term development of agencies through providing a fund of insights and information which can inform an agency about its own history. Many agencies operate as though they have no history. Each project or decision is made in isolation, as though it were the first in the organisation's history. If the organisation is lucky some of those making decisions may at least call on their memories of past mistakes and thus inform their decision making. There are certain common obstacles to good institutional learning:

(i) *The charity or voluntary culture:* the misplaced assumption that money spent on training, research, archives, in house publications and the like, is a luxury. The 'we are too busy doing the job' response to any serious review of the effectiveness, efficiency and impact of the work. As a consequence, lessons are not learnt from the past successes as well as failures and as many wonderful success stories as failures are lost.

(ii) *The lack of a learning culture:* one participant in an INTRAC workshop recalled that he was interrupted in his office whilst reading a book and greeted by the comment, 'oh, you're reading–I thought you were working.' There is little time or resources allowed for agency staff to reflect on their own experience or to record it or share it with others. Training budgets are very small and donors known for their generous funding of training and research in the South allow virtually no such resource for themselves. It is assumed that staff arrive with all the sufficient skills and knowledge on the day they start work, and that this will suffice until they resign or retire!

(iii) *The competitive market:* many agencies are wary of collaborating with research projects, or of sharing their experience because they regard all other agencies as being in competition with them for funds. Furthermore some agencies have rules against sharing information with those outside in case bad publicity harms their fundraising image.

(iv) *Funding pattern:* certain types of funding profile make it difficult for agencies to use their income for the purposes of institutional learning. For example, many cofunding schemes providing government funds to NGOs or sponsorship schemes where funds are tied to specific projects do not allow sufficient resources for the good use of agency experience.

(v) *Fear of exposure:* the nature of many generalist agencies in the North is one of the factors which dilutes the real level of experience they are able to demonstrate. The lack of professional specialists and tendency for staff to concentrate upon geographically organised desks mitigates further against a sharing of experiences across areas. In the South, low resource levels, multiple job holding, are amongst the factors which reduce the real knowledge of many NGO workers of the problems they face. Rather than admit to any form of ignorance, it is safer to avoid answering difficult questions about the detail of the work.

(vi) *The uncritical culture:* this is often tied to the 'charitable' or voluntary origins of many NGOs. These are often coupled with a religious or other conviction that good works are valid in their own right and that to do good must be right and to challenge this is through evaluation is both unnecessary and unacceptable.

(vii) *Eclecticism—'jack of all trades master of none':* in a recent review of UK NGOs (Pratt *et al.* 1992), it was clear that most were what could be described as 'generalist' agencies, in that they did not specialise in any particular form of development. The pattern of NGOs being generalist is common throughout the North and South. This means that there are few professional staff with specialised knowledge and experience who might be able to bring together experiences in their field.

There are no easy solutions to these problems, and indeed some go well beyond the scope of the present book. Certain paths are open to agencies which include the following:

• encouraging thematic research and 'meta-evaluations' which utilise the findings of individual evaluations to reach broader conclusions;

• publication of more evaluations, and publications based on research which use evaluations;

• programmes to encourage greater 'in-house' learning through seminars, staff exchanges, staff crossing between departments,

• using staff from one partner organisation in the evaluation of another partner;

• greater specialisation by agencies, to allow them some degree of comparative advantage in relation to certain developmental approaches and methods.

Conclusion

In terms of the process involved in the evaluation of social development, one of the major problems identified is the lack of consistency to be found within NGOs. This lack of consistency is illustrated through a gap between 'NGO theory and NGO practice'. Many NGOs espouse participation, democracy and other liberal values, but the practice of evaluation continues to use top down approaches.

While it could be said that NGOs have progressed in terms of understanding the debates and concepts related to the evaluation of social development, there is, however, a continuing lag between ideal practice and common practice. It is still not easy to identify cases whereby NGOs have engaged in a consistent and thorough process of evaluation geared to the needs of social development. The challenge still to be confronted by a NGO community committed to the concepts of social development is to refine and operationalise more frequently alternative approaches to evaluating social development programmes.

Box 5.2
Checklist for Undertaking Evaluation

(1) Is the purpose of the evaluation clearly set out and agreed by all parties in the TOR?

(2) Is it clear who will receive the report and what they have to do with it?

(3) Is there a management plan for acting upon the report?

(4) Is there provision for follow-up once the evaluation report is completed?

(5) Is there provision for discussion, negotiation and further action based on the evaluation between the different actors (stakeholders)?

(6) Are the methods of disseminating the findings of the evaluation appropriate to the different stakeholders? (eg. for non-literates, different languages, etc.)

(7) Is there provision for discussion of the initial findings before the report is written? This is particularly important where evaluation teams leave the site of the evaluation before the complete their report.

CHAPTER SIX

CONCLUSION

1. THE EMERGENT AGENDA

Reflecting on the Practice

In the concluding comments on each of the Case Studies in Chapter 3 and in the substantial Chapters 4 and 5, in which we reviewed and analysed the more practical aspects of the evaluation of social development, we have sought to pull together some of the more common and important issues related to this form of evaluation. An overall conclusion of this analysis of the practice must be to underline the evident pluralism of social development evaluation; there is no single view, no single methodology and no single set of rules. Social development encompasses a broad range of essentially qualitative processes and activities, which cannot be understood or accompanied by any single, snap-shot instrument. It is important that all of those involved in the evaluation of social development can draw upon a broad repertoire of approaches, techniques and instruments. Another conclusion would draw attention to the central importance of negotiation in the whole social development evaluation process. Negotiation is crucial to the whole process; it helps to demythologise the distant instruments of evaluation, it informs and empowers the non-professionals and it increases the probability that outcomes will be both acceptable and intelligible to all involved. Other more specific observations that we could make as a whole on the practice illustrated in the text include:

(i) The debate has only just begun on the whole issue of the time and cost involved in evaluating social development programmes. Each of the Case Studies in Chapter 3 illustrated the critical importance of taking these two factors into account; the Zimbabwe study in particular details the quite exhaustive and time-consuming nature of such evaluations. For the purist, cost and time are not so critical; we must achieve an authentic process and produce an outcome which eschews the snap-shot but paints the 'full-picture'. Others would agree that it is important to get the process right, but at what cost and how long will it take? Already some argue that all these 'participatory processes' lead to over-complication, to stultifyingly slow progress and to decision-making processes which are so extended and non-directional that nothing appears to happen. None of these observations is entirely right. Factors of cost and time must be brought into the equation, but then who is to determine 'value'? We still await a systematic costing of an 'authentic process of social development and its evaluation' and when we have one, the debate will be joined. In an age which is increasingly strident on 'targets', 'profitability' and 'cost-effectiveness' it will be interesting to see how development practitioners confront such 'values' when witness to the complex demands of social development programmes.

(ii) The great majority of the presentations made to the Workshop, which have been incorporated into the text but not published separately, attested to the continuing challenge not only to maintain but even to establish a balance between the 'qualitative' and the 'quantitative' in social development evaluation. Time and again presentations emphasised the qualitative nature of social development, only to tip towards the quantitative in its evaluation. Perhaps a major explanation here is the simple fact that so many development professionals come from an essentially empirical approach to research and evaluation and, while cognisant of new emerging paradigms, essentially lack the ideological preparation of practical experience to develop the more qualitative sides of programme evaluation. In particular it was noticeable how few were able to construct a 'qualitative' base-line view of the context in which they operated and thus to develop an appropriate evaluation design from that base. The 'process' of social development cannot be understood in purely quantitative terms, but for the moment evaluators' strengths appear to lie in this area. Qualitative phenomena such as 'social change', 'levels of consciousness' and 'participation', for example, continue to present formidable conceptual and methodological problems in their evaluation; some projects have broken the mould, others are experimenting imaginatively but a large number are still feeling their way in this new practice.

(iii) Like all evaluation exercises, but perhaps more so given its 'value-laden' nature, the process of social development evaluation is subject to a whole series of external influences. In the many presentations made to the Workshop references to matters such as the 'influence of external donors', 'external expectations' of the evaluation, 'donor style' and 'accountability to donors' were not uncommon. In the world of NGOs and social development there will always be closer and more day to day contact between donors and their partners than, for example, in some mammoth five year construction project; after all the donors see themselves as 'part of the process' and want to be involved. It is this being involved and determining how best to do it which appears to be the issue and there are no immediate models nor universal rules for this interface. But the influence of the donors is there, it is constant and it will bring with it the shifts in donor thinking. More recently, and this was evident in the case studies, there has been a shift towards giving greater emphasis to the 'management' of development projects; it would appear that many donors are tiring of this seemingly endless processes of social development and they would now wish to bring it within a more conventional managerial grasp. There is an understandable reluctance in some quarters to 'let the process run'; equally there is a lack of recognition that the 'change' implied in a process of social development cannot be instant and overnight and that the chance of structural re-alignment which such projects seek might be lost in an eagerness for managerial control.

On the basis of the presentations made an overall conclusion would be that the 'emerging evaluation paradigm' in practice has yet to take a firm grip. In general terms the presentations were strong on concepts and notions, but less so on evidence of a distinctive evaluation approach to social development projects. In one respect, however, this form of evaluation is beginning to take shape; and that is in terms of the overall 'approach' to evaluation. Chapter 4 shows how the many projects reviewed are beginning to break-down the overall complex process of social development into a series of discrete stages or steps and to use this breaking-down as a structure for evaluation. At the level of conceptualisation and basic focus, the notion of the process nature of social development evaluation seems now to be on quite solid ground. But the practice is less focused or consistent and there is a feeling that many projects are less confident in terms of taking the next step. Given the emergence in the past few years of several practical guides to the taking of this next step, as identified in Chapters 2 and 5, there would appear to be a major issue of 'preparation' or 'training'. Perhaps what is needed is less workshops and seminars discussing what the evaluation of social development is all about and more emphasis on direct training and involvement in the practicalities of the process.

Finally the practice as illustrated in the presentations made to the Workshop underline what has been a central argument throughout the two Workshops; that the interpretation of social development is directly related to the approach of its evaluation. The book on the earlier workshop outlined an interpretation of social development which has served as the basic focus for our work in this area; not service or welfare provision but a process of change and transformation which seeks to redefine and renegotiate the economic, social and political relationships which are at the core of any society's development. Curiously in some of the practice we can note an imbalance between the notion of social development and an evaluation approach more linked to the quantitative aspects of provision. A major practical task still remains of how to construct the balance and how to evaluate the process.

2. NEGOATATING THE CHANGING REALITY

The current debates that surround the evaluation of development projects are embedded in wider debates about authority, legitimacy, transparency and accountability. At the risk of polarising discussion, one can identify two opposing viewpoints. At one extreme there is the acceptance by both theoreticians and practitioners of some objectively verifiable universe which can be ordered and reproduced. At the other extreme is the acceptance by other theoreticians and practitioners of a much less structured and ordered universe. The one is based on assumptions of predictability as enshrined in a scientific ability to land people on the moon, for example. The other is based on assumptions that structures and organisations are 'emergent', that knowledge and understanding are negotiated (see Long and Long 1992). The one gives rise to an understanding of evaluations as being capable of providing objective assessments of performance through various forms of analysis, whether economic or sociological, rooted in the elaboration of more sophisticated 'scientific' methods and instruments. There is an assumption that greater sophistication will provide a greater ability to predict and based on that, the development of a toolbox that can be universally applied. The other recognises the unpredictability of change, the uncertainty of attributions of causation, and the partiality of knowledge. One focuses on the production of products that can be generally communicated in a language which stands apart from particular realities and which can eventually be universally replicated. The other focuses on processes that are context specific and which recognise that attributions of success (or failure) depend on the values of the various stakeholders in their analysis of goals and objectives.

It should be obvious that the focus which the authors attempt to elaborate in this text is one that gives priority to process, negotiation, and contextual analysis. As Carlson et al. point out in a recent critique of the effectiveness of aid:

> The evaluation function has to take into account that reality is not a 'given' thing to be discovered by a detached scientist: rather, reality is 'constructed' by actors and those who are involved in the particular activity. (Carlson et al. 1994:200)

With them we agree that evaluation should be perceived more as a tool for learning rather than as a tool for management. But we would argue that its importance for institutional development, and for rethinking organisational development, should not be consigned to a secondary position. It should be an important part of a renegotiated management in which issues of partnership and transparency gain increased relevance and in which the relationship between 'donors' and 'beneficiaries' ('givers' and 'receivers') can be re-thought. Perhaps NGOs are in a better position to take this agenda forward because the constraints under which they operate are less complex than those of governments and multi-lateral aid agencies.

The current importance attached to achieving value for money in aid projects, disguises some of these more basic issues. There is a need to find out whether or not resources committed in the name of development are actually worthwhile; a need to ensure efficiency and effectiveness in implementation; and a need to control expenditure and direction, given the moral agenda which underpins thinking about aid. Justice, equity and good government vie with economic growth in the moral agendas of the various protagonists. The causal relationship between aid and economic growth remains dubious.

Recent studies are at best equivocal on whether aid is effective (see Mosley, Harrigan and Toye 1991, Lipton and Toye 1992) and some would argue that it is more 'supply' than 'demand' driven–there is a great deal of money chasing very few good projects–which is likely to compromise any evaluation based on demand led theories and methodologies. Bauer argues that there is little evidence to indicate that external donations are required for economic development (Bauer 1992). The tools that economists have used to measure change (macro-economic and political economic analyses, cost-benefit and cost effectiveness analyses) have been largely based on concerns for competitive efficiency. Where welfare concerns have been important, it has apparently proved difficult to develop tools that are any more than crude instruments. There is often an assumption that a high degree of certainty exists and that careful rational calculation is feasible. The assumptions required, in the absence of reliable data, quickly take the economic calculations outside the realms of reality. As Carlson et al. suggest, 'economic analysis is not able to capture the reality of developing countries' (1994:6).

The Capture of Reality?

But can reality ever be captured? Some would argue that current, inadequate methods for measuring impact and effectiveness can be improved by the development of more elaborate techniques for analysis. But this is in danger of taking them beyond the realms of all but a privileged few who can understand their complexities. Others would argue that they can be complemented by other sorts of analysis that are less demanding in their need for reliable statistics and which are more 'qualitative' in nature (ethnographic studies, organisational and situational analyses, case studies, etc.). Gradually thereby a more complete picture of reality can be built up.

The assumptions that lie behind such evaluations are of systematic and objective analyses which investigate the design, implementation and results of development projects in order to provide information on efficiency, effectiveness, impact, sustainability and the relevance and appropriateness of objectives. Armed with that information, managers will be able to make more appropriate decisions.

But if we accept that reality is 'emergent', that development projects provide an 'interface' between different understandings (both divergent and convergent) of reality, then a very different appreciation of the tools to be used in evaluation ensues. The assumptions which underlie analyses should then themselves become the primary objects for systematic investigation. This does not mean that the tools already developed should be ignored or put to one side in favour of an alternative set of tools, nor that they cannot be developed further. Rather there is a need to re-position them in terms of the different priorities which emerge from this different understanding. The thinking behind the development of a different set of priorities then requires that a more reflexive understanding of the nature of the relationship between donors and beneficiaries be developed, as issues such as justice, equity, participation and good governance necessitate the renegotiation of the ways in which the methodologies are applied. Growth is not the only, nor even the most important, issue in the development equation.

There is no doubt that evaluations should help improve project performance, should ensure that information is available at the right time and in a digestible form, and should provide information to those who are committing resources, both physical and financial. There is also no doubt that development is about enhancing productivity and that a distinction between economic and social development based on the former's concern with productivity and the latter's concern with welfare cannot and should not be drawn. The artificial divisions that have been raised are largely based, not on different subject matters, but on different ways of perceiving and analysing reality. The distinction is between those who think that reality can be captured and those who see reality as 'emergent', rather than between economists and the rest.

Evaluations and Emergent Project Realities

Recognising the emergent nature of project reality, we maintain that evaluation should be seen as an ongoing process associated with the negotiation of an 'acceptable compromise' between the various stakeholders in the context of particular projects and programmes over a particular period and in a particular context. We also maintain that evaluations inevitably involve moral and political agendas. These moral agendas are enshrined in one form or another in the different emphases that donors place on such issues as participation, equity and justice. Evaluations have traditionally been dominated by donors who have tried to set the direction for the process of project development. We have often assumed that those donors operate with a singular purpose, in the same way that we have assumed that 'beneficiaries' have come from homogeneous communities. It is obvious that even in the smallest organisations, whether governmental or non-governmental, that individuals have different sets of priorities and see things in different ways.

If we see reality as 'emergent' and the process of project implementation as participatory then evaluations serve as centripetal foci around which that emergent reality can revolve. They create the legitimacy for further action and the authority to encourage commitment. They become processes for the achievement of objectives set through team work for the achievement of higher quality as well as higher quantities in terms of enhanced productivity. Evaluations can thus become the poles around which discussion about quality management can revolve. Macdonald and Piggott, in a recent analysis of TQM (Total Quality Management) practices in the West, cite Dr. Kaoru Ishikawa, who they describe as, 'a major contributor to the development of quality management in Japan' (Macdonald and Piggott 1990:6). According to Macdonald and Piggot, Ishikawa recognises quality management as a revolutionary management philosophy characterised by the following strategic goals:

1. Seek quality before profits.

2. Develop employees' infinite potential through education, delegation and positive support.

3. Build long-term consumer orientation, both outside and inside the organisation.

4. Communicate through the organisation with facts and statistical data, and use measurement as motivation.

5. Develop a company-wide system focusing all employees on the quality-related implications of every decision and action at all stages of development of the product or service, from design to sales.

(Macdonald and Piggott 1990:6-7)

They go on to state that the four key requirements of the TQM process are these:

- There must be a common understanding of quality and the need to change.

- Management must develop operating principles and values which create the environment for continuous improvement.

- Management must create the organisation and provide the resources to support the improvement process.

- Everyone must contribute to the end product or service used by the customer.

(Macdonald and Piggott 1990:192)

If we strip these statements down and turn them around, they might provide the basis for linking current thinking in management circles with that associated with the development of a more participatory appraisal and evaluation process. The essential shifts concern the role of 'managers' and the distinctions made between producers and consumers. In development projects we are obviously not dealing with a capitalist enterprise but we are concerned with achieving better quality 'products'. There is an assumption that interventions in the name of development should have a positive impact. As with the management of quality there is need to establish a set of milestones, or benchmarks whereby those assumptions can be tested and progress, in terms of improvements in quality of life, can be assessed.

Everyone wants to see better quality but its assessment remains positional and qualified by the context in which it is recognised; the need for sanitary latrines and safe drinking water, for example, may not be foremost in the minds of villagers struggling to sustain rather precarious livelihood strategies. The alignment of donor and beneficiary priorities, so that both feel a commitment to each others agendas, becomes an important objective. The focus on participation, on good governance and on gender in particular in many Northern aid programmes, highlights this. An emergent reality means a constant struggle to get these issues on many agendas.

Possibilities for the Negotiation of Moral Agenda
The distinctions being drawn throughout this book, between what might be termed 'traditional' evaluations and 'interpretative' evaluations assume that it is possible to re-focus methods and subordinate them to a shifting moral agenda. Interpretative evaluations recognise the emergent nature of social action in which reality is 'constructed' by the all actors involved at the

'interface' which is the development project. Interpretative evaluations begin with the assumption that those involved jointly construct the reality of the project and negotiate solutions to the problems of value that arise from it. While cost utility analysis provides all stakeholders with the opportunity to assess the results of alternative courses of action according to their own value judgements, it is a beginning rather than an end; the starting point for those stakeholders to address options, develop priorities and clarify objectives together. The backdrop for such analyses are emergent, for example, in such foci as those being developed in participatory appraisal methods.

Such analyses provide opportunities for re-thinking costs and benefits, effectiveness and utility, but where the 'target group' identified through the project process and the various stakeholders who emerge in terms of that targeting, take centre stage. Through such analyses, winners and losers will be identified, power differentials perceived, and realistic bases for future achievements negotiated. The logical framework approach, if utilised in a participatory manner, provides an opportunity on which to hang questions of objectives, directions, achievements and their measurement. Both quantitative and qualitative measures might be used, but when and where will be determined by the context.

Strengthening Institutions

While evaluations are still very largely driven by the agenda of the North, that agenda is changing in response to a variety of influences which are emergent in the priorities set for resource transfers. An increasing concern to ensure institutional development and sustainability requires different questions about project management and project implementation to be asked. Aid agencies are still primarily interested in assessing the impact of development interventions, understanding how and why objectives have been or have not been achieved, and understanding more clearly the differences between costs and benefits. But attempts to focus on participation, on community-based activities, and then on sustainability and maintenance of assets, necessitates a shift towards organisation and institutional strengthening as prerequisites for the successful application of resources; and a shift from delivery of products, to laying appropriate foundations for supporting appropriate resource flows. This requires the development of many forms of partnership and a recognition that different organisations have different roles to play.

INTRAC, for example, has been involved in developing an approach to organisational assessment which moves beyond the mainstream management literature and tries to relate different aspects of NGO developmental and organisational features. Underlying this form of organisational assessment is the relationship between the performance of developmental programmes and the nature of the sponsoring organisation, and further, the relationships or links beween these and client groups (whether individuals or community based organisations), government, other NGOs or networks. Figure 6.1 tries to represent the outline of this by illustrating the triangulation of information on criteria and indicators for these three areas.

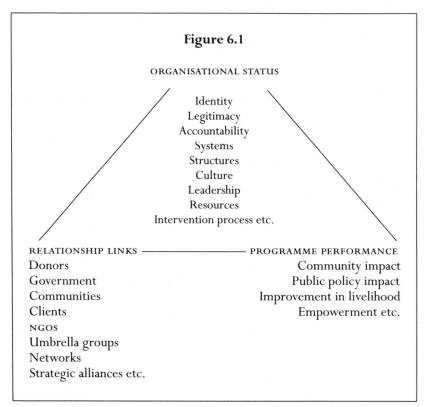

Figure 6.1

ORGANISATIONAL STATUS

Identity
Legitimacy
Accountability
Systems
Structures
Culture
Leadership
Resources
Intervention process etc.

RELATIONSHIP LINKS ——————— PROGRAMME PERFORMANCE

RELATIONSHIP LINKS	PROGRAMME PERFORMANCE
Donors	Community impact
Government	Public policy impact
Communities	Improvement in livelihood
Clients	Empowerment etc.
NGOS	
Umbrella groups	
Networks	
Strategic alliances etc.	

The recognition of the importance of organisational or institution building is leading several agencies to move away from project-centred to organisational-centred concerns. This has encouraged an emerging literature of strategies for institutional and organisational development, assessment and strategies for intervention, capacity building, monitoring and evaluation (see Fowler 1992). It has been argued that earlier concerns of social development activists have now been legitimised in orthodox development thinking through the concern over governance and civil society. This has further encouraged the support for organisations as an end in themselves, as a part of plural or civil society, as well as the delivery mechanisms for the views of people and of services to them (see Clayton 1994).

Those Who Create Should Sustain

An interpretative appraisal would aim to ensure that the obligations for sustainability were met both by 'donors' and 'beneficiaries'. The development of partnerships requires more than the mere transfer of resources; it implies the commitment by all parties to the joint sustainability of activities and/or assets. This has implications for project funding in terms of four or five year project cycles. These have not to date been given much thought in governmental terms and it is likely that efforts to ensure sustainability will imply longer term commitments and more open funding arrangements, with evaluations being part of an ongoing process to steer a course which can ensure continuous readjustments. As with the PROMESA case study analysed earlier, evaluation becomes an on-going strategy for reflection and motivation which feeds into programme planning and enhances transparency–people know what they are involved in and take some responsibility/ ownership of that set of activities.

While it might not be possible to develop a common framework for the evaluation of those development projects which are concerned with activities which are not just aimed at enhancing economic productivity, it is possible to talk in terms of a logical framework. There is no reason to confine current attempts to use logical framework techniques to decision makers who represent donor agencies. There is every reason to believe that it can be utilised as a participatory tool for the development of local level planning and implementation capacity, for the generation of appropriate indicators of achievement and for planning ways in which negotiated objectives can be achieved. The question that remains is whether external donors are prepared to subordinate their own objectives to the wider debate that would be required and whether the established bureaucracies which administer the various aid budgets can re-orient themselves for these new challenges. The use of techniques such as the logical framework technique provide opportunities for the development of templates which do not rest on the vicissitudes of personnel but which provide opportunities for building up an institutional memory that transcends individual involvement and commitment to projects.

The Need for Data and Information

In pursuit of more effective appraisal and evaluation methods, it has often been the complaint that evaluations have been inhibited by the lack of adequate and relevant base line data. While it is always important to know where one has come from in order to analyse the various milestones that one has passed, it is important not to fetishise such statistics and information. They are usually only available in global terms, at very aggregated levels and are surrounded by qualifications as to their accuracy. Or they are very individual and subjective accounts from particular perspectives. In the unlikely event that there is base line data that can provide direct opportunities to reflect on current conditions, it is likely that it has only marginal relevance for current concerns about direction. If it is accepted that reality is emergent then this data and information provides individuals and organisations with arguments to justify their own preoccupations. It will be used selectively and to buttress particular perceptions.

The need for timely, appropriate and accessible information is undeniable. But again the establishment of an interpretative and participatory framework suggests that participants themselves will be the arbiters of what information is required. The assumption that somehow the more information that one has, the more able one is to make decisions, rests on the dubious premise that everything can and should be known. If a participatory exercise has resulted in the establishment of a set of realistic objectives accompanied by the selection of appropriate indicators for their measurement then the sorts of information that will be necessary will emerge from that process. Only then can a realistic base line data set be developed. Many evaluations call for the development of a set of data and a body of information that can serve as a base for measuring accomplishments in the future. If, as is common, these evaluations take place towards the end of a process, they chart the way forward. In this sense, the end is the beginning and the terminal evaluation has been transformed into an initial appraisal in an on-going process of qualitative change and the illusion of time-bound, discrete interventions is shattered.

Whither the Evaluation of Social Development?
At the end of a particular process which has spanned five years and involved two workshops are we any further forward in our understanding of how to evaluate social development, or even clear about what we mean when we talk about process projects which often involve activities which are not amenable to measurement? We hope that we may have contributed in small part to the ongoing debates. Our journey of discovery has been paralleled by many others.

There is evidence that the complex issues that surround the development of a participatory agenda which has underpinned our own efforts, are becoming more central in the debates of the large and influential organisations at the forefront in establishing the official development agenda. The World Bank, for example is currently putting considerable effort into understanding what participatory development can mean (World Bank 1992). UNDP also has taken considerable pains to understand how large donor organisations can better support participatory development and is in the process of rethinking its own role. The Development Assistance Committee of the OECD has endorsed a set of orientations on participatory development and good governance, and the Development Centre of the same organisation is currently undertaking a project to understand how participatory development through local institutions might be promoted. Many of the UN agencies are committed to the elaboration of a participatory agenda., from the FAO's People's Participation Programme to the UN Capital Development Fund's exploration of participatory eco-development (UNCDF 1993).

The operationalisation of these concepts remains problematic, but a continued focus on such things as evaluation, impact assessment and the measurement of outputs rather than inputs has led to the beginnings of a major re-think about the nature of the aid relationship in general. The emphasis on the project approach is being questioned. There is recognition that the world is composed of multiple and complex realities which need to be understood and negotiated if progress is to be made. Emphases on accountability, on institutional development, and on more democratic information flows suggest that a movement to more demand led solutions is being sought. There is an increased recognition that if progress is to be sustained then the solutions are context specific. The lessons learned from the past suggest that a focus on institutional development, and on the development of more appropriate management practices, is shifting the development effort from one which has been dominated by the supply of services, to one in which the development of capacity to utilise and absorb external resources is more important. Participatory evaluations can help in the identification of strengths and weaknesses in the practices of both donors and recipients and thus assist in the development of more appropriate and successful practice. The tasks associated with restructuring aid relationships are formidable, but the enthusiasm and commitment demonstrated by all those involved at all sorts of levels would seem to suggest that directions and associations can be shifted. The current focus on impact assessment and on measuring outputs rather than inputs contributes to this shift in perception and on the establishment of a restructured practice.

SELECT BIBLIOGRAPHY

AGKED and MISEREOR (1991) *Evaluations in the Churches' Development Cooperation: A Workbook for Implementing Partner Organisations and Support Agencies*, AGKED and MISEREOR, Aachen and Stuttgart.

Ahmed, V. and Bamberger, M. (1989) *Monitoring and Evaluating Development Projects: The South Asian Experience*, Economic Development Institute of the World Bank, Washington.

Aga Khan Rural Support Programme (1993) *Institutional Maturity Index: A Process Approach for Participatory Monitoring and Evaluation of Village Organisations in Gilgit*, by Tetlay K.A. and Mahmood S., AKRSP, MER Section, Gilgit, Pakistan.

Apthorpe, R. (1992) *Making Evaluation Matter: A Teaching Paper on Evaluation in Practice*, Institute of Social Studies, The Hague.

Bamberger, M. (1989) 'The Monitoring and Evaluation of Public Sector Programs in Asia: why are development programs monitored but not evaluated?', *Evaluation Review* Vol. 13, No. 3, pp. 223-242.

Banuri, T. (1990) 'Development and the Politics of Knowledge: A Critical Interpretation of the Social Role of Modernization Theories in the Development of the Third World' in F.A. and S.A. Marglin (eds.) *Dominating Knowledge: Development, Culture and Resistance*, Clarendon Press, Oxford.

Bauer, P.T. (1992) *Equality, The Third World and Economic Delusion*, Weidenfeld and Nicolson, London.

Beaudoux, E. *et al.* (1992) *Supporting Development Action: From Identification to Evaluation*, Macmillan, London.

Bhatnagar, B. and Williams, A.C. (eds.) (1992) 'Participatory Development and the World Bank: Potential Directions for Change', World Bank Discussion Paper No.183, World Bank, Washington.

Brokensha, D.W., Warren, D.M. and Werner, O. (1980) *Indigenous Knowledge Systems and Development*, University Press of America, Lanham.

Brown, D. (1991) 'Methodological Considerations in the Evaluation of Social Development', *Community Development Journal*, Vol. 26, No. 4.

Carlson, J., Köhlin, G., Ekbom, A. (1994) *The Political Economy of Evaluation: International Aid Agencies and the Effectiveness of Aid*, Macmillan and St. Martin's Press, London.

Casley, D.J. and Lury, D.A. (1982) *Monitoring and Evaluation of Agriculture and Rural Development Projects*, Johns Hopkins University Press, Baltimore.

Casley, D.J. and Kumar, K., (1987) *Project Monitoring and Evaluation in Agriculture*, World Bank, Johns Hopkins University Press, Baltimore.

—— (1988) *The Collection, Analysis, and Use of Monitoring and Evaluation Data*, World Bank, Johns Hopkins University Press, Baltimore.

Cernea, M. ed. (1985) *Putting People First*, Oxford University Press, Oxford.

Chambers, R. (1985) 'Shortcut Methods of Gathering Social Information for Rural Development Projects' in M. Cernea ed. (1985).

Chambers, R., Pacey, A., and Thrupp, L.R. (eds.) (1989) *Farmer First: Farmer Innovation and Agricultural Research*, Intermediate Technology Publications, London.

Clayton, A.J. (ed.) (1994) *Governance Democracy and Conditionality: What Role for NGOs?*, INTRAC, Oxford.

Cochrane, G. (1979) *The Cultural Appraisal of Development Projects*, Praeger, New York.

Coleman, G. (1992) 'Monitoring and Evaluation in Agricultural and Rural Development Projects: Lessons and Learning', *Journal of International Development*, Vol. 4.

Coninck, J and Riddell, R. (1992) 'Evaluating the Impact of NGOs in Rural Poverty Alleviation: Uganda Country Study', ODI Working Paper 51.

Conway, G.R., and Barbier, E.B. (1990) *After The Green Revolution: Sustainable Agriculture for Development*, Earthscan, London.

Cornia, A. *et al.* (1987) *Adjustment with a Human Face*, UNICEF, Clarendon Press, Oxford.

Cornwall, A., Guijt, I. and Welbourn, A. (1992) 'Acknowledging Process: Challenges for Agricultural Research and Extension Methodology', Overview Paper II for IIED/IDS Beyond Farmer First Workshop, 27-29th October 1992, Brighton.

Croll, E. and Parkin, D. (eds.) (1992) *Bush Base: Forest Farm: Culture, Environment and Development*, Routledge, London.

Damodoran, K. (1991) 'Measuring Social Development through the Development of Qualitative Indicators', *Community Development Journal*, Vol. 26, No. 4.

Davis-Case, D'Arcy (1989) *Participatory Assessment, Monitoring and Evaluation: A Field Manual*, Community Forestry Unit of the FAO, Rome.

Davis-Case, D'Arcy (1990) *The Community's Toolbox: the Idea, Methods and Tools for Participatory Assessment, Monitoring and Evaluation in Community Forestry*, Community Forestry Unit of the FAO, Rome.

Donnelly-Roark, P. (1993) *Re-inventing Bureaucracy for Sustainable Development: How Large Donor Organisations can Better Support Participatory Development* (Draft), UNDP, New York.

Epstein, T.S. (1988) *A Manual for Culturally-Adapted Market Research in the Development Process*, RWAL Publications, Bexhill-on-Sea.

—— (1992) 'How Participatory Research and Development Can Be Conducted in a Cost- and Time-Effective Way', paper presented to G.A.P.P. Conference on Participatory Development, July 1992.

Featherstone, M. (ed.) (1990) *Global Culture: Nationalism, Globalization and Modernity*, Sage, London.

Ferguson, J. (1990) *The Anti-Politics Machine: Development, Depoliticization and Bureaucratic Power in Lesotho*, Cambridge University Press, Cambridge.

Feuerstein, M-T. (1986) *Partners in Evaluation: Evaluating Development and Community Programmes with Participants*, Macmillan, London.

Fowler, A. (1992) *Institutional Development and NGOs in Africa: Policy Perspectives for European Development Agencies*, INTRAC, Oxford.

Ford, R. *et al.* (1992) *Sustaining Development through community Mobilization: A Case Study of Participatory Rural Appraisal in The Gambia*, Clark University and Action Aid The Gambia.

Freidman, J. (1992) *Empowerment: the Politics of Alternative Development*, Blackwell, Oxford.

Gasper, D. (1987) 'Motivations and Manipulations: Some Practices of Project Appraisal and Evaluation', *Manchester Papers on Development*, Vol. 3, No. 1. pp.24-70.

Ghai, D. and Westendorff, D. (eds.) (1994) *Monitoring Social Progress in the 1990s: Data Constraints, Concerns and Priorities*, UNRISD, Avebury, Aldershot.

Guba, E.G. and Lincoln, Y.S. (1989) *Fourth Generation Evaluation*, Sage, London.

Hancock, G. (1989) *Lords of Poverty: The Power, Prestige, and Corruption of the International Aid Business*, Atlantic Monthly Press, New York.

Handy, C. (1988) *Understanding Voluntary Orgnizations*, Penguin Books, London.

Harding, P. (1991) 'Qualitiative Indicators and the Project Framework', *Community Development Journal*, Vol. 26, No. 4.

Hilhorst, J.G.M. and Klatter, M. (eds.) (1985) *Social Development in the Third World: Levels of Living Indicators and Social Planning*, Croom Helm, London.

Howes, M. (1991) 'Linking Paradigms and Practise: Key issues in the Appraisal, Monitoring and Evaluation of British NGO Projects', revised edition of paper presented at the Development Studies Association Conference, Swansea, 12 September 1991.

IFAD (1985) *Monitoring and Evaluation: Guiding Principles for the Design and Use in Rural Development Projects and Programmes in Developing Countries*, IFAD, Rome.

IIED*RRA Notes* (1988–), published periodically by the Sustainable Agriculture Programme of the International Institute for Environment and Development, London.

IIED/IDS (1992) *Beyong Farmer First: Rural People's Knowledge, Agricultural Research and Extension Practice Workshop, Proceedings*, Institute of Development Studies.

Kabutha, C., Thomas-Taylor, B.P. and Ford, R. (1990) *Participatory Rural Appraisal Handbook*, World Resources Institute, in collaboration with Kenya's National Environment Secretariat, Egerton University and Clark University.

Khan, Akhter Hamid (1983) *The Works of Akhter Hamid Khan*, 3 Vols, Bangladesh Academy for Rural Development, Comilla, Bangladesh.

Korten, D.C. (1990) *Getting to the 21st Century: Voluntary Action and the Global Agenda*, Kumarian Press, West Hartford.

Korten, D.C. and Klauss, R. (1984) *People Centred Development*, Kumarian Press, West Hartford.

Lazarev, G. (1993) *Towards Participatory Eco-Development: A Thematic Study Review*, United Nations Capital Development Fund, New York.

Lipton, M. and Toye, J. (1991) *Does Aid work in India? A Country Study of Official Development Assistance*, Routledge, London.

Long, N. and Long, A. (eds.) (1992) *Battlefields of Knowledge: The Interlocking of Theory and Practice in Social Research and Development*, Routledge, London.

Marglin, F.A. and S.A. (eds.) (1990) *Dominating Knowledge: Development, Culture and Resistance*, Clarendon Press, Oxford.

Macdonald, J. and Piggott, J. (1990) *Global Quality: The New Management Culture*, Mercury, London.

Marsden, D.J. and Oakley, P. (1990) *Evaluating Social Development Projects*, Oxfam, Oxford.

Morris, T. (1991) *The Despairing Developer: Diary of an Aid Worker in the Middle East*, I.B. Tauris, London.

Mosley, P., Harrigan, J., and Toye, J. (1991) *Aid and Power: The World Bank and Policy-based Lending*, Routledge, London.

Muir, A. and Riddell, R. (1992) 'Evaluating the Impact of NGOs in Rural Poverty Alleviation: Zimbabwe Country Study', ODI Working Paper 52.

Nadler, D.A. and Tushman, M.L. (1988) *Strategic Organisation Design: Concepts, Tools and Processes*, Harper Collins, USA.

Neefjes, K. (1992) *Participatory Environmental Assessment and Planning for Development,* the results of a workshop held in Cambodia in December 1992, Oxfam, Oxford.

Nichols, P. (1991) *Social Survey Methods: A Fieldguide for Development Workers*, Oxfam, Oxford.

Oakley, P. (1991) *Projects with People*, ILO, Geneva.

ODA (1993a) *Project Evaluation: A Guide for NGOs*, ODA, London.

―――― (1993b) *Social Development Handbook*, ODA, London.

OECD (1993) *DAC Orientations on Participatory Development and Good Governance*, OCDE/GD (93) 191, Paris.

Oxfam (1985) *The Field Directors' Handbook*, Oxfam, Oxford.

Patton, M.Q. (1978) *Utilization-focused Evaluation*, Sage, London.

―――― (1980) *Qualitative Evaluation Methods*, Sage, London.

―――― (1982) *Practical Evaluation*, Sage, London.

―――― (1987) *Creative Evaluation* (2nd edition), Sage, London.

Paudyal, D.P. (1991) 'Monitoring and Evaluation Mechanism of Agrarian Reform and Rural Development in Selected Asian Countries' *Asia Pacific Journal of Rural Development*, Vol. 1, No. 1.

Pirsig, R. (1992) *Lila: the Metaphysics of Quality*, Vantage Press, London.

Porter, D. *et al.* (1991) *Development in Practice: Paved with Good Intentions*, Routledge, London.

Pottier, J. (ed.) (1993) *Practising Development: Social Science Perspectives*, Routledge, London.

Pratt, B.S. and Loizos, P. (1992) *Choosing Research Methods: Data Collection for Development Workers*, Oxfam, Oxford.

Pratt, B.S., Hailey, J., Sahley, C., and James, R. (1992) *A Review of UK NGO Support for Small Enterprise Development Programmes*, INTRAC, Oxford.

Pretty, J.N. and Chambers, R. (1992) 'Turning the New Leaf: New Professionalism, Institutions and Policies for Agriculture', Overview Paper for IIED/IDS Beyond Farmer First Workshop, 27-29th October 1992, Brighton.

Rahman, A. (1984) *Grass-roots Participation and Self Reliance*, Oxford and IBH Publishing Co., New Delhi.

Reed, M.I. (1989) *The Sociology of Management*, Harvester Wheatsheaf, Hemel Hempstead.

—— (1992) *The Sociology of Organizations*, Harvester Wheatsheaf, Hemel Hempstead.

Richards, H. (1985) *The Evaluation of Cultural Action: An Evaluative Study of the Parents and Children Program (PPH)*, Macmillan Press, London.

Richards, P. (1985) *Indigenous Agricultural Revolution: Ecology and Food Production in West Africa*, Hutchinson, London.

Riddell, R. (1990) 'Judging Success: Evaluating NGO Approaches to Alleviating Poverty in Developing Countries', ODI Working Paper 37.

Robinson, M.A. (1991) 'Evaluating the Impact of NGOs in Rural Poverty Alleviation: India Country Study', ODI Working Paper 49.

—— (1992) 'Churches Auxilliary for Social Action (CASA): Phase III Integrated Rural Development Programme.' International Workshop on the Evaluation of Social Development, Amersfoort, The Netherlands, 11-15 May 1992.

Rondinelli, D. (1983) *Development Projects as Policy Experiments*, Methuen, London.

Save the Children Fund (1994) *Assessment, Monitoring, Review and Evaluation Toolkits*, SCF, London.

Scoones, I. and Thompson, J. (1992) 'Rural People's Knowledge, Agricultural Research and Extension Practice: Towards a Theoretical Framework', Overview Paper I for IIED/IDS Beyond Farmer First Workshop, 27-29th October 1992.Brighton.

Spitz, P. (1992) *Participatory Evalution of Rural Development Projects*, IFAD, Monitoring and Evaluation Division, Special Studies, Report No. 0385, Rome.

Spitz, P. (1993) 'International Fund for Agricultural Development: Experiences with People's Participation', in Bhatnagar B. and Williams A.C. (eds.) *Participatory Development and the World Bank*, World Bank Discussion Paper No. 183, Washington.

Stebbins, W. and Shani, Abraham B. (1989) 'Organisational Design: Beyond the Mafia Model', Organisational Dynamics, American Management Association.

Stephen, F. (N.D.) *NGOs–Hope of the Last Decade of this Century*, Bangalore (mimeo).

—— (1991) *Search News*, Vol. 4, Issues 2 and 3, Bangalore, India.

Tendler, J. (1982) 'Turning PVOs into Development Agencies: Questions for Evaluation', USAID Program Evaluation Discussion Paper No. 12.

UNDP (1993) *Human Development Report*, Oxford University Press, New York.

Uphoff N. (1986) *Local Institutional Development*, Kumarian Press, West Hartford.

Uphoff, N. (1991) 'A Field Methodology for Participatory Self-evaluation', *Community Development Journal*, Vol. 26, No. 4.

—— (1992) 'Monitoring and Evaluating Popular Participation in World Bank-Assisted Projects', in Bhatnagar B. and Williams A.C. (eds.) *Participatory Development and the World Bank*, World Bank Discussion Paper No. 183, Washington.

—— (1992) 'Participatory Evaluation of Rural Development Projects: Lessons from Experience and Implications for Donor Agencies', paper prepared for Panel on Monitoring and Evaluation of ACC Task Force on Rural Development, Report No. 0385, Monitoring and Evaluation Division, International Fund for Agricultural Development, Rome.

Van Ufford, Q., Kruyt, and Downing, T. (eds.) (1988) *The Hidden Crisis in Development: Development Bureaucracies*, Free University Press, Amsterdam.

Verhelst, T.G. (1990) *No Life Without Roots: Culture and Development*, Zed Books, London.

White, S.C. (1991) 'Evaluating the Impact of NGOs in Rural Poverty Alleviation: Bangladesh Country Study', ODI Working Paper 50.

Wildavsky, A. (1979) *The Art and Craft of Policy Analysis: Speaking Truth to Power*, Little, Brown and Co., Boston.

World Bank (1991) *The Social Dimensions of Adjustment Integrated Survey: A Survey to Measure Poverty and Understand the Effects of Policy Change on Households*, World Bank, Washington.

Wright, S. (ed.) (1994) *The Anthropology of Organisations*, Routledge, London.

Zadek and Evans (1993) *Auditing the Market: A Practical Approach to Social Audit,* Traidcraft with the New Economics Foundation, Newcastle and London.

List of Case Studies presented to the Workshop

1. Alejandro Accosta, *A Case Study: The International Centre for Education and Human Development, CINDE, Colombia and the Evaluation of the Programme to Improve Education, Health and the Environment (PROMESA).*

2. Veronica Brand and Cosmas Wakatama, *Evaluating Social Development: A Case Study of the Catholic Development Commission, Zimbabwe.*

3. Ayele Gebre Mariam, *The Evaluation of Social Development Projects: Dello Development Project, Bale Administration Region, Ethiopia.*

4. R. Monhanraj, *The Process of Evaluating Social Development, Prajwala, India.*

5. Mark Robinson, *Churches' Auxiliary for Social Action (CASA): Phase III Integrated Rural Development Programme.*

6. Chris Roche, *A Case Study on an Evaluation Process in Mali.*

7. Dominique Steiner, *Some Elements on Self Evaluation.*

8. Tove Wang, *Redd Barna–Zimbabwe Country Programme Review.*

9. Alfredo Coronel, *Analysis of the Evaluation and Monitoring System for the Income Generating Project in Villa El Salvador, Lima, Peru.*

List of Participants on the International Workshop on the Evaluation of Social Development 1992

1. Alejandro Acosta, CINDE, Colombia; 2. Sr. Veronica Brand, Catholic Development Commission, Zimbabwe; 3. Susan Coe, World Vision, UK; 4. Mary Convill, Christian Aid, UK; 5. Alfredo Coronel, Rescursos, Peru; 6. Martin Dütting, MISEREOR, Germany; 7. Ivar Evensmo, DIS, Norway; 8. Tony Fernandes, CEBEMO, The Netherlands; 9. Karoline Frey, Aga Khan Foundation, UK; 10. Doris Galinski, Giessen, Germany; 11. Ayele Gebre Mariam, Ethiopia; 12. Gaim Gebreab, Norwegian Church Aid, Norway; 13. Dieneke de Groot, ICCO, Netherlands; 14. Ana Marie Groot, SNV, Netherlands; 15. Mick Howes, Institute of Development Studies, University of Sussex; 16. Heinz Knüvener, MISEREOR, Germany; 17. Reinhard Koppe, AGKED, Germany; 18. David Marsden, Centre for Development Studies, University College of Swansea; 19. R. Mohanraj, PRAJWALA, India; 20. Bert Noordergraaf, ICCO, Netherlands; 21. Peter Oakley, Save the Children Fund (UK), Colombia; 22. Frances O'Gorman, CEAR, Brazil; 23. Margaret O'Grady, Christian Aid, UK; 24. Brian Pratt, INTRAC, UK; 25. Maria Ribeiro, SCF Ireland; 26. Chris Roche, ACORD, UK; 27. Mark Robinson, Overseas Development Institute, UK; 28. Dominique Steiner, GAP, Belgium; 29. F. Stephen, SEARCH, India; 30. Tove Wang, Redd Barna, Zimbabwe; 31. Cosmos Wakatama, Catholic Development Commission, Zimbabwe; 32. Ton van Zuthphen, CEBEMO, Netherlands.

INTRAC NGO Management and Policy Series

OTHER TITLES

Institutional Development and NGOs in Africa: Policy Perspectives for European Development Agencies (INTRAC NGO Management and Policy Series No. 1)

Alan Fowler, with Piers Campbell and Brian Pratt

Institutional development is recognised as an important element in projects and programmes dedicated to the sustainable alleviation of poverty, the promotion of gender equity and achieving social justice for marginalised populations. Commissioned by the Netherlands Organisation for International Development Co-operation (NOVIB), the report provides an overview of NGO institutional development in the context of sub-Saharan Africa. Its primary purpose is to assist European NGOs to formulate policies and strategies towards the institutional development of the NGO community on the sub-continent.

ISBN 1-897748-00-0
PRICE £5.95 + P&P
52PP; JULY 1992

Governance, Democracy and Conditionality: What Role for NGOs? (INTRAC NGO Management and Policy Series No. 2)

Edited by Andrew Clayton

This publication addresses the issues of good governance and conditionality from the perspective of both Northern and Southern NGOs. It will be of interest to those engaged in the management of NGO programmes, policy-makers, and those involved in lobbying and campaigning. The publication is based on the papers and case studies from the INTRAC workshop in Amersfoort, the Netherlands in June 1993. The workshop brought about fifty participants together, from both Northern and Southern NGOs as well as bilateral and multilateral agencies, in order to reflect on the implications of this new policy agenda for NGOs. Key issues covered in the publication include: NGO positions regarding conditionality; the role of NGOs in promoting good governance; the relationship between development NGOs and human rights groups; Southern perspectives on donor conditionality; NGOs and working with Southern governments; and people's conditionalities. The case studies draw on the experiences of NGOs in Africa, Asia and Latin America, and cover a wide range of issues concerning the role of NGOs in civil society, advocacy, legal reform and democracy movements. The book also contains an introduction, and a paper that sets the wider context of the debate, as well as a select bibliography.

ISBN 1-897748-01-9
PRICE £7.95 + P&P
144PP; MARCH 1994